Power Trips

Norman Rawlings

Copyright © 2019 by **Norman Rawlings**

All rights reserved. No part of this publication may be reproduced, distributed or transmitted in any form or by any means, without prior written permission.

Village Books Publishing
1200 11th St, Bellingham WA
Bellingham, WA 98225

Publisher's Note: This is a work of fiction. Names, characters, places, and incidents are a product of the author's imagination. Locales and public names are sometimes used for atmospheric purposes. Any resemblance to actual people, living or dead, or to businesses, companies, events, institutions, or locales is completely coincidental.

Book Layout © 2017 BookDesignTemplates.com

Power Trips/ Norm Rawlings. -- 1st ed.

Power Trips

Norman Rawlings

For my dad, Robert H. Rawlings, Sr.

Acknowledgements

Thanks to my editor, Sabine Sloley, for her critical eye and professionalism in looking through the several versions of manuscripts. Thanks also go to Candee Blanc and the entire team at Village Books for their work and support in getting this project to completion.

I want to thank my wife, Teresa, for her constant support throughout this project. There were moments when writing all this down seemed a little ***too*** cathartic. I thought that maybe it should remain on my laptop, within my journal, on a half of a dozen flash drives, and twice as many scraps of paper, hidden from the world. But over time, she provided the extra push and encouragement in suggesting that some of these stories and thoughts actually might help others.

Shout out to my children, Maxwell and Morgan Rawlings. They are the inspirations to so many of my stories, thoughts, and actions. I've said it before, and I'll say it again: My life began when yours did.

Lastly, I wish to acknowledge all of the characters in my life that inspired the writing of these memoirs, essays, stories, etc. However our relationship turned out, whether it is still prospering, whether it has died on the vine years ago, or if it is somewhere in between, I still hold you all very close to my heart. I wish for you all the peace and happiness that life has to offer.

Preface

I was originally going to call this book "Left Turns" because of the references throughout the chapters to making wild, senseless decisions that took me down dark alleys. But then I thought that "Left Turns" was a stupid name for a book. Maybe people would think that it was a tribute to the sport of NASCAR or something.

Then I was going to name it "Quit Drinking, Meeting Adjourned." There is a thread of alcohol that weaves through these pages and Lord knows, I've had my own struggles with the stuff. But I realized I have a bad habit of oversimplifying life's many complicated, deeply emotional events. And while I think there is some practical wisdom in starting off a journey or life-changing experience with a simple decision, I felt "Quit Drinking, Meeting Adjourned" was an insulting title. For some people, it takes incredible bravery to show up to an AA meeting in the first place, much less to quit drinking altogether. So I quickly dismissed that choice. It was offensive and flippant. When I was younger, I didn't mind being offensive. Partly because I thought I was right all the time, but mainly because I was an asshole. But since I'm not really a flippant person and I never liked insulting people (then or now), it's best to leave that title on the editing room floor.

I considered calling the book "Channeling My Inner Bob" in reference to my father and my brother, both named Robert; they make appearances in some of these stories, especially my father, who played a significant role in my life and to whom I dedicate this book. But then I found out about the blogs, social media pages, and YouTube videos called *Channeling My Inner Bob Ross*. Ross was an American painter and art instructor who gathered some fame on TV and who taught us all how to paint "happy little trees."

I re-read the stories I wrote. I tweaked them here and there, flipped their order around, and then left them alone for weeks on end as I tried to come up with a better title. I even added a piece from my previously published book, *Barstool Jesus: The Saltier Side of Grace*, in order for it to flow a little better. I told my wife, Teresa, that I was having trouble figuring out what to call this book. She knows my heart and my mind better than anyone, and she also knows the stages and the players of my life and knows where I want to go and—more importantly—where I've been. She knows all the dark alleys I've gone down and what I've put my family and friends through as I left the warm glow of their company to walk off into the shadows alone. She thought about it for a few days and then gave me the title that had been eluding me from the beginning: *Power Trips*.

In my life there have been instances and events where I have struggled for control, for power, over myself and my surroundings. These events are pinned on the atlas of my life like little yellow and red thumbtacks that a college student might pin to a map of the world indicating places they long to travel to or have visited already. The difference is that my thumbtacks represent the relationships with my family, my children, and the people brave enough to call themselves my friends (and the ones who used to but don't anymore). They also symbolize a complex relationship between my father and me, the hurtful distance (both physically and emotionally) I carelessly put between myself and my son and daughter, and the wild, impetuous course I set upon to escape my troubled past. As I journeyed from one thumbtack to another on this map, I tried to remind myself that not every new place I came to sheltered a suitcase with a ticking bomb, waiting to blow me to pieces. And I tried not to leave a bomb with my name on it for someone else to find. I failed at that sometimes, and I regret that failure deeply.

Yet despite the ugly emotional thicket that sometimes is my life and my decisions, some places on the map are marked by wonderfully charged occurrences and soulful, heartfelt exchanges. There are pinpoints representing exhilarating memories, deeply passionate love affairs, and glorious victories with teammates. There also exists laughter so genuine, pure, and raucous that I lost control of bodily functions and didn't care one damn bit about drawing too much attention. "We might be laughin' a bit too loud, ah. . . but that never hurt no one."

As with most things, however, there's the other end of the spectrum: thumbtacks representing big steaming mounds of shit where bad decisions, bad breaks, and bad people sent me veering off course. That's the deal you make with life, sometimes. If you're going to walk through the garden, you've got to be ready to step in a pile of what makes that garden grow. And ladies and gentlemen, I have done my fair share of gardening.

Despite my initial cynicism and suspicion about my worth in this world, I eventually managed to control my self-confidence and self-doubt, two wildly unpredictable bullies that have wreaked havoc on my heart and mind ever since I was a young boy. And while I have traversed tens of thousands of miles in my lifetime, moving between two points on the globe—up and down one stretch of the same lonely highway between the Canadian border and Portland, Oregon—in search of happiness, peace, and the perfect bottle of red wine, I recognized that these thumbtacks didn't always represent a positive experience. Sometimes they illuminated the presence of the demons that I allowed to run uncontested within me. For a while, the pins in the map of my life reflected a great distance between each positive, happy placement until one Norman couldn't recognize the other due to the emotional span between them. But over time I've managed to shrink the distance between the constructive coordinates on my map, and now look more fondly on them rather than feel guilty about being happy during those moments. You would be surprised how awkward happiness can be to those that haven't seen a lot of it.

I began to better understand who I was, who I am now, and who I want to be going forward. I don't know if my vision has become clearer so I can look at all of the events of my life (including the ones yet to come) with a softer perspective, or if I have settled into a more judicious approach to my life so I can plot a healthier course toward the days I have remaining. The jury is still out on those questions. What I do know is that without some very good people who stood next to me when all others went screaming for the hills, I would most certainly still be lost within a bottomless bottle and sucking in the dirty, polluted air of a regretful existence.

And so. . . back to the title of this book. The stories within these pages are those colorful little markers—the thumbtacks on my map. The trips between pins are my day-to-day observations. And the knowledge from these lessons is the power that fuels my life going forward.

Good or bad, right or wrong, metaphorically or literally... these are my power trips.

D.T., the C-Bomber, and Elvis

Some years ago I spent an hour each week sitting with complete strangers. My drinking had gotten out of control, so I took society's recommendation to meet with other temperate souls at some Alcoholic Anonymous meetings and talk about what losers (and quitters) we were becoming.

At this anonymous meeting with other anonymous members was an old man who had tried to sober up for years. Each time I saw him he reminded me of Mark Twain's quote about trying to quit smoking. Twain wrote, "To cease smoking is the easiest thing. I ought to know. I've done it a thousand times." This old-timer told our group he had stopped and started drinking over five hundred times in his life, but he only really remembered two attempts. As a result of his lifetime of drinking, quitting, and starting again, his body had developed a constant state of tremor; his hands and the lower part of his face were always twitching. The tics and twitches seemed to be the physical reminders that he had lost control of himself and his life.

"This is my last try, my last chance," he said. "I've lost three wives, I can't remember the last job I've held for longer than a year, and I haven't spoken with my children in God knows how long." He mumbled the last part under his breath with his chin buried in his chest. He looked at the faces watching him curiously, sympathetically, or painfully, his quivering hands wrapped around the knobs of his knees. He began recounting the series of events that brought him to that cramped space in the back storage room of a dirty office building, and as he outlined the spider web of paths that took him to his own private purgatory, it became increasingly difficult to tell if the shaking was from sobriety or from the earthquake of emotions rolling through him. In the interest of anonymity, I will call this man "D.T."

D.T. always worked off the same template for his stories, but the tales contained different characters and backdrops. He told a slightly different version each time we saw him. One version had him as a young father working insanely long hours—over ninety per week—as a longshoreman. His two daughters grew up seeing their father only for a few hours on Sundays or in the occasional glimpse in the middle of the night after he had stumbled home. They might pass each other in the hallway at 3 a.m., one on his way home from the bar and the other on her way to the bathroom. At a very early age, D.T.'s daughters recognized the smell of cheap brown liquor mixed with sweat and cigarette smoke. It smelled like the guy they were supposed to call "Daddy". As D.T. would tell the group later, this odiferous awareness would serve one daughter well when she grew older and started dating. For the other daughter, the lack of awareness would prove disastrous in her choice of a husband.

In another version of D.T.'s story, he came home earlier than expected from work and found his wife sitting in the backyard with a strange man. D.T. was never the type of guy who got too confrontational. He couldn't remember if he had ever been the "in-your-face" type of person. I understood that sort of classification. That much liquor in the system for years can either erode the sensitivity of the heart, making you numb to things that would normally rile up other men, or it can inflame the heart by pumping it full of jealous toxins and spurring you on to violence. So, in D.T.'s case, because he did not know what to do, he did nothing. He just watched his wife introduce the guest as a member of the church she went to religiously and the one that D.T. avoided like the plague. The guest was also a lawyer—a very specific type of lawyer – that would prove to be of great significance to D.T and his marriage a few weeks later.

The final version of D.T.'s story was a lonely one. The backdrop was an old studio apartment with a thirty-year-old sofa bed covered with coffee stains and caked with musty memories. There also existed a loud, coughing refrigerator stocked full with bottles of vodka, beer, and one very expensive, very old magnum of champagne. The latter never got opened despite the dozens of times he ran out of his other poisons of choice and "had" to have something to drink. In one of the last meetings he attended, in front of complete strangers, he confessed that he dumped every bottle of alcohol in that broken refrigerator down the sink or the toilet, but he still had that one bottle of champagne. He took it out and rolled it between the palms of his hands on the nights when the demons came to whisper into his ear that life is easier when the glass is full.

He recalled, under his breath and through a gravelly whisper, that that bottle of champagne was a gift from his father when he married his high school sweetheart, the same woman with whom he had two beautiful daughters and who had finally given up on trying to stop him from killing himself four ounces at a time. Ironically, more than going to meetings or making regular calls to his sponsor or even taking his daily dose of Disulfiram, rolling that bottle between his palms was the one simple exercise from his ugly past that quelled the hissing reminders that he was still one step away from the edge of the cliff. As D.T. once put it, "That bottle is the last bullet from the first gun."

A few weeks after he told the final version of his story, he stopped coming. That was disconcerting to me, because if you stop coming it usually means something bad has happened. I still pray for D.T. now and then.

Another attendant of our weekly get-togethers was a young woman who could not have been more than eighteen or nineteen years old. That's a complete guess based on the limited range of her vocabulary and the airiness of her voice. Despite her juvenile conversational style, she didn't appear uneducated or dense. In fact, I recall her being pretty sharp and alert. It was just that her mannerisms indicated innocence rather than experience, and you don't seem to get that too often with non-teenagers.

Somehow, she must have been aware of this classification because all she wanted was to get the group to label her as a street smart, hardcore woman with a razor's edge. To accomplish this, she used the word "cunt"—a lot. She seemed to revel in making the other members of the group bristle. Even among the more salted, hardened outcasts, the c-word still provides a societal hiccup that reeks of revulsion. A friend once said to me, "Of the more than 170,000 words in the English language, it is the *one-time* employment of *that* single word that will destroy an otherwise blissful marriage."

So she described her friends as a bunch of cunts whose hypocrisy was apparently only bested by their self-righteousness. The more she dropped the c-bomb, the more the people in the group seemed to cringe and write her off. One middle-aged guy (whom I will call Charley) had had enough. He cleared his throat and interrupted her in mid-sentence. "You know. . . no one is defining you the way you want them to when you talk like that. No one is looking at you like some mysterious, brooding artist or edgy heroine of the streets. You're broken, just like the rest of us. But you are here because you want to be, not cuz you have to be. So stop acting like the world is against you and own up to the one simple fact that seems to be escaping you."

There was a long silence punctuated by a piercing stare from the C-Bomber. With eyebrows raised in a slight state of shock, and her mouth still open from the last words she had been rambling on about, she stared back at Charley until a tear leaked out of the corner of her eye. "Which fact is that?" she whispered.

"The fact that you want to be someone you are not." Charley stood and refilled his Styrofoam cup with cheap coffee. As he poured, she glared at him like he just slapped her face with the backside of a leather work glove. Charley mumbled, almost to himself, as he sat back down in his folding chair, "I'd bet every dollar I have left in my pocket against every dollar left in yours that we all would like that person more than the bitch you're trying to be right now." He sipped his coffee and crossed his legs and raised his eyes to her. A silent tension filled the room for a full two minutes.

"You don't know shit," she finally said, her voice cracking.

Charley snorted out a laugh and rolled his eyes. "Yeah, well. . . I'll be the first one to admit that." He took another sip of his coffee and stared back at her with sleepy, compassionate eyes.

I watched this exchange quietly. I had a world of things to tell this young woman. I wanted to convince her how much I understood her rage, and and how foreign and yet familiar it was. I wanted to tell her that pretending to be a character from a TV show or a movie in lieu of not knowing who you are and what purpose you serve on this earth only made things worse. I didn't doubt the validity of her anger. Lord knows, I've had nine kinds of it in my life and it went in eleven different directions and none of it made any damn sense. But I just wanted to ask her what parts of her life *did* make sense. I wanted to ask her if she had a few healthy things in her life that she trusted, and that she could fall back on to feel safe when things started to go haywire. It seemed a logical question. When you're getting dumped on in a rainstorm the first thing you normally do is look for shelter, right? So, where was her shelter? What healthy emotional, physical, or spiritual place would she retreat to when things got bad? Where, in her head and her heart, was "dry land"? After all, I suppose that is what we were all doing there in the first place. After a while, the C-Bomber went dark and didn't say much. She didn't speak out much after that, but she didn't leave either. I took that as a good sign.

The last member of our group was an intimidating man, standing over six and a half feet tall, who called himself Hatchet Jack Rose. Hatchet Jack was a proud Native American whose name wasn't really Hatchet Jack Rose, but I'll call him that to cover the anonymity requirement. The name he gave us in that room was an alias anyway. It probably wasn't the first time someone showed up to an AA meeting using an alias, but I bet those other people didn't have as cool a persona as Hatchet Jack Rose.

Hatchet Jack used to work at circuses and carnivals throwing knives, axes, and hatchets at targets from a distance. As if that weren't interesting enough, he would do it dressed like Elvis Presley while singing classic Elvis songs. Every alcoholic has a story. The trick is not to glorify the story and romanticize the carnage that booze can bring to people's lives, but there was *no* way the people in that little room were going to let this guy walk out the door without hearing more of his story.

So we listened and laughed along with Hatchet Jack as he described his life. We were captivated as he told us about each town he traveled to and each performance he gave under the big top. He had a bit of a quiet swagger to him, so imagining him dressed up like the King of Rock and Roll wasn't all that difficult. The group smiled at each story and laughed out loud when Hatch Jack punctuated the end of each story with "Thank you. . . thank you very much" in a perfect Elvis, southern-drawl baritone. The smiles slowly melted, however, when Hatchet Jack described each little tavern on the outskirts of each little town that he would sniff out after the show was over. No one recognized him in the taverns because he wouldn't wear his costume, and the faces in these taverns never looked up anyway. They were always buried in the bottom of their glasses looking for something they lost long ago, or staring into space to see something that was never there in the first place.

Jack told us that he drank to create something, not to remember or forget anything. He drank so his mind would come to life. He drank in hopes that the days he spent pretending to be something would somehow morph him into a respectable *someone*, if only in his own mind. He called himself "the quietest drunk in history," because he never talked to anyone when he drank but just sat at the end of the bar and sipped his life away while dreaming of better days. It was only when his body started to fail him that he realized this quiet process of creating a life was killing him from the inside out. So he saw a doctor in the next town and got the news he was expecting. He sold all of his Elvis jumpsuits, pawned all of his axes, hatchets, and throwing knives, quit drinking cold turkey, and got in his old GMC truck and drove out west until he ran out of money.

He stopped at the first town that "didn't smell funny" to him and got a steady job at a hardware store. He used the internet for the first time in his life to look up the nearest AA meeting, and that was where we first met him: the one-and-only Hatchet Jack Rose, the blade-slinging Elvis Presley of the Midwest shit-town carnival circuit who could now get you a pretty good deal on drill bits and wallpaper hangers.

A new job took me away from the area, but through a social media contact I found out later that Hatchet Jack Rose died of liver cancer. He was twenty-two months sober into his new life. The post from my fellow meeting member said it all: "Hatchet Jack Rose has left the building."

These three souls (and many others) discovered their brokenness among strangers in that little room. We recognized that within our fractured life existed more fractures, and then more fractures splitting off from those fractures. Our drinking days became like a defective jigsaw puzzle whose pieces weren't exactly shaped to fit one another but managed to show the picture or tell a story anyway. All you had to do was shove together a few days, or round off some edges. Under an umbrella of anonymity we laid out our stories on the coffee tables before us. Our alcoholic lives were all a little Picasso-esque, but the images we created together were eerily familiar. That's what too much booze does to some people. It can distort the peaceful, harmonious vision of one's life and turn it into a rough, imperfect sketch filled with blurred lines and blotched images; indistinguishable to those that are affected by it and unrecognizable from the flawless design from the steady hand of God.

That's the nature of human nature, I suppose. We try to jam a square block of human experience into the perfectly precise circle and we end up with an infinity puzzle with pieces missing, wrongly shaped, and poorly decorated.

But we make do and we learn. D.T., the C-Bomber, and Hatchet Jack (along with a million others) have seen life's puzzle put together much cleaner and easier by those that do not have drinking problems or those that may have overcome their addictions . They tried to understand how it was done, and juxtaposed the pieces of their own puzzle against pieces they admired. But the images they were working with and the design in their minds' eyes were flawed and warped; tangled, melted misrepresentations of how they thought the puzzle of life was supposed to look. So they took another drink and hoped that one more sip would make the image come into focus a little more clearly or make it disappear entirely.

In that little storeroom—and in thousands of other rooms just like it all over the world—men and women finally recognize this frustrating cycle. And with time, patience, and the help of their fellow quitters, they start to realize that the glasses they were looking through may have been the problem in the first place.

"Tell Me Lies, Tell Me Sweet Little Lies..."

I was seven years old when my mom and dad packed up my brother, sister, and me, and moved sixteen hundred miles east to a little town in the Midwest called Willmar, Minnesota. We were only there for about two years, and why we moved there was a mystery to me at the time.

We had been living rather happily (or so I thought) near other family members in Shelton, Washington, a small logging town in the Pacific Northwest. Shelton is where I remember growing up. I played Little League baseball there, I played high school football there, I graduated from high school there, much of my family still lives there to this day, and I have relatives buried in the great state of Washington. So to me, Minnesota seemed like a wild hair of an idea. It appeared to be "let's see what happens when we press this button" type of thing. In other words, it was a wicked left turn on what had seemingly been an otherwise straight and narrow path.

I thought my parents chose Minnesota like someone would choose a different kind of beer when the normal one they drank at their neighborhood pub had ran out. It seemed like a flippant decision. It shows the tremendous gap of understanding little kids have on the important decisions their parents face every day. So, in a clear and blatant affront to what *I* wanted, my father packed up his family and headed out east to work on a turkey farm in the land of ten thousand lakes.

Minnesota, to a small boy, was a land right out of a Jack London novel. I had never seen that many spots to swim or knew that snow could fall that often or get that deep. Once, my father had to shimmy out of the kitchen window to shovel snow away from the front door so we could get out of the house!

Back in Washington State, the mosquitoes were pesky little annoyances that showed up every now and then while we were camping; a couple of little bites, you slapped on some calamine lotion and presto, you were back in business and the bumps were gone. In Minnesota, however, mosquitoes are a whole separate deal. They are often referred to as the state bird, because some are the size of freaking paperclips. They float menacingly around the campfire waiting for small pets or young children to wander off on their own before swooping in to carry them off to their lair. One bite from those blood suckers and you end up scratching yourself right down to the bone.

In Minnesota every grownup seemed to have a garage full of toys: snowmobiles and fishing boats, and a whole family set of ice skates hanging on nails in the mud room. Everyone fished and hunted. Everyone played outside. Even when the temperature and humidity soared to suffering levels or the thermometer dropped to sub-zero conditions, the good people of Minnesota were found outdoors doing something exhilarating. You had to admire that kind of insanity and commitment to having fun. Later in my life, a different kind of commitment toward having fun would nearly cost me everything, but for the good folk of Minnesota, playing outdoors was how friends and family bonded together.

I don't have a lot of memories of this time of my childhood. I'm not sure why that is other than the fact that it was almost forty-five years ago. Maybe my foggy memory is due to the blows to the head I received on the football field or the punches I collected in the dark alleys I staggered down. But every now and then, I remember Willmar. I don't really recall the house we lived in or the school I attended. I don't remember my room or what kind of cars my parents drove. I can't think of the names of teachers, neighboring cities, or even friends I had when I was that age. But I remember the snow, and the water, and the back trails through corn fields. I remember seeing my first ice shanty on a frozen lake and how amazingly prehistoric a Northern Pike looked to me when my dad pulled it out of the water. I don't recall running away screaming, but my dad told me that is what I did when he threw that fish at my feet.

Willmar, Minnesota, is also America's Turkey Capital of the World. Jennie-O is headquartered there, as are about forty other large farms that hatch, grow, inoculate, and ultimately slaughter those hideously ugly yet incredibly yummy birds we have all come to know and love as the symbol of our holiday gluttony. My dad managed one of those farms.

My dad managed three barns, each about the length of a football field and nearly the same width. The first was dedicated to male adult birds or "toms." They are rather intimidating-looking creatures. Some stand nearly 2 ½ to 3 feet tall and—to a six year old—looked like squat, feathered aliens with baggy chins and crooked necks. For those of you who have only experienced turkey between two pieces of wheat bread smothered in cranberry sauce, let me square you up on a little tip: full-grown male turkeys have a murderously insane mean streak. They are also ridiculously fast runners. They would chase me down and peck away at me if I happened to fall.

Wild turkeys have actually been clocked at twenty-five miles per hour, which seems hilariously ironic considering they don't fly. I'd normally be somewhat impressed by this piece of inane trivia, but all I can think about is that there is someone, somewhere, in the world clocking turkeys with a stopwatch. I wonder how they got them to run. And I also wonder, what job did that guy have *before* he started timing turkeys?

The second barn was populated by young hens; harmless-looking females without all the nastiness and voracity of their adult male counterparts and also void of all the ridiculous decoration. And at the risk of sounding insensitive toward poultry, they are all carbon copies of one another. They drift in currents like schools of fish. They don't cackle or scream like adult toms sometimes do. For the most part they just lay eggs, poop, and stand around waiting to eat. There is no political hierarchy with the hens. They mill around the yard inside the barn waiting for nothing in particular to happen and aren't overtly surprised when it does.

The third barn was full of turkey chicks; tens of thousands of little balls of yellow fur pecking away innocently and without a care in the world. Walking among them was like walking ankle-deep in a sea of yellow fuzz. With the adult toms I had to be careful not to trip and fall, because they could descend on you and peck you to pieces. However, with the chicks I had to walk tenderly so as not to squash the little farts. They were all so Hallmark-card cute as they bee-bopped around, peeping and chirping in vocal registers that could break glass. They had zero idea that one day they would grow up to be food. Then again, so will the rest of us, I suppose.

Every Saturday morning my dad woke up my brother and me at 5:00 a.m. and we would suffer the long walk from the house to the first barn with its ten thousand toms. The three of us made a lengthwise sweep of the building, looking for dead turkeys that had been trampled, or pecked, or had simply given up among the constant throng of their brotherhood. It was a gruesome task. When I wasn't hiccupping puke into my mouth at the stench of the turkey shit I was wading through, the funk of a decomposed twenty-pound bird would certainly send the bile northward. As a result of this kind of exposure as a small boy, I don't really have a gag reflex anymore. There have been days when I certainly needed one.

Not long after we left Willmar and returned home to the Pacific Northwest, I began to quickly forget that little excursion to the Midwest. But as the years progressed and I became more mature I started to wonder why we ended up leaving Washington State in the first place. Even at such a young age, I recall asking my parents why we lived in Willmar for only a few years. I would grill my parents now and then what prompted them to move us all out there and why we moved back to Shelton so abruptly. They would just mumble something about "it was a good job" and then quickly change the subject.

What I didn't understand about Willmar—and what I found out much later in life—was that sometimes adults lie to their children to hide some very unflattering realities. I don't think they lie to them just to be pricks or to screw up their heads or something. They generally wrap up the farce in a neat, cozy little rationalization and serve it up with a soft voice, a tousle of the hair, and a large twisty cone at the local Dairy Queen. The truth they were hiding was that moving to Willmar was a risky move for a family of five. I had been told, growing up, that the few years we spent in Minnesota was for a good job and perhaps a strategic career move. While that was true, it was also a gamble my father took to keep bread on the table because things weren't going so well back home. Once I first got to Willmar, I was miserable. In my very young mind, I was furious with my father for moving us away from family and the only friends that I had. I somehow convinced myself that Willmar wasn't home. It was never going to be home. And all the warm turkey pot pie and countless swimming holes was not going to change my opinion.

Ultimately, as kids grow up and become more cognizant that they are not the center of the universe and that life isn't a constant stream of butt powdering, bubble baths, and outdoor barbeques, the lies we find out about don't end up to be all that painful. In fact, the little fibs that I used to tell my own son and daughter when they were young no longer seem as treacherous to their development as my psyche made them out to be.

For instance, I remember telling my kids that the local Chuck E. Cheese restaurant was closed. . . forever. . . because of a fire. I also told them that their favorite tape of Barney the Dinosaur (the one that had been played so often the theme music started to seep into my subconscious) had been loaned to some poor kids who didn't have cartoons to watch. And the whopper that I still cringe about was that the exhaustively long children's book they insisted I read to them every night was "at the book cleaners," and we'd have to settle for this short little ten pager about a Brown Bear and What He Saw.

More than likely, these little dishonesties have all been discovered by my kids for what they really were: simple solutions to uncomfortable conundrums. I didn't know what to say to them. I didn't want to tell them that if I saw that six foot rat in that shitty pizza parlor again I was going to harm him or myself. I didn't want them to know I couldn't stand that purple dinosaur's voice anymore. And I didn't have the heart to admit Daddy was so very tired and that while I'd swim through oceans of fire to keep them safe, making up voices for every character in *Mrs. Frisby and the Rats of Nimh* just wasn't going to happen that night.

And so, in the same way, my parents told me and my siblings that Willmar would be fun, and fine, and an adventure because they didn't know what else to say. They were trying to keep their life going forward. I get it. I finally get it.

Now that I'm an adult I don't criticize things as much as I used to. And I think that, in time, the lies I've been told when I was young about how life works for adults—how men and women were supposed to treat each other and how parents raise their kids—will out themselves as simple lessons on perspective. I like to think that my own choices have become instructive experiences rather than some deep-seated pathological problems (which still may be the case, I guess). "Life lessons" is soft, warm, and approachable phrase that depicts a healthy recognition of past mistakes and an honest attempt to implement change. But the only soft, warm, and approachable thing about the word "pathological" is the couch you will find yourself reclining upon at $125 per hour. So, since my definitions are cheaper, I will chose trust them more.

Rationalize much?

Victor Karl

My mother, for nearly 50 years, was a nurse. For a great deal of that time she worked at a convalescent center in my home town of Shelton, Washington. When I was in high school I used to drop in to see her and say hello to some of her residents. I always got a kick out of talking to them and hearing their stories. One of them in particular was a gentleman named Victor Karl. That's not his real name of course, but since I've recently gotten in trouble with publishing some real names in some of my stories I decided that everyone I know is now going to have a pseudonym, whether they need one or not. My sister, for instance, is now called Dr. Charlie Lichtenstein and my brother is Gus the Wonder Lizard.

Anyway, Victor (at that time) was the most senior resident in the building. He was 105 years old and was what my dad liked to call "full of piss and vinegar." I would sit next to him and listen to him drift back in time to perhaps a moment he would spend with his own son:

"DAVID? DAVID...IS THAT YOU?"

"No, Mr. Karl, I'm Norm. I'm Nurse Rawlings' boy. How are you feeling today?"

"DAVID?"

"No, no sir...my name is Norm. I came and visited you yesterday. Remember? We talked about Korea and how they recently closed Mill #5 and when you used to pitch horseshoes? Remember?"

"GO TO HELL! WHERE'S DAVID?"

This was our standard introduction nearly every day. However, once we got through this routine Mr. Karl would fall into a monologue about the state of humanity through his eyes, his life in the logging business, his deadbeat grandchildren who didn't have the time of day for him, and the three sons he buried many years ago (one of them being David). He seethed about the wife that kissed him goodbye one morning, drove out to the corner store for his cigarettes and never came back. He still could taste her berry cobbler and "shit black coffee." I pause to note that Mrs. Karl did eventually come back to Victor. She was there to lay him to rest at the end of his days. Victor always loved younger women. She was 86.

I think of Victor every now and then. As a young man, I found him entertaining and fascinating as he regaled me with the same story in the same angry tone every time I spoke to him. He was mad about the "pansy ass bastards wanting to save every tree from here to Christmas" and the "sonsabitchin' politicians" and how there didn't seem to be one honest thinker in the history of American Government. Victor also didn't think much of "Ben Henry…that bastard…he couldn't set a choker to save his goddamned life." I giggled most of the time. I nodded a lot. It really didn't matter how I reacted because Victor wasn't talking to me anyway. There always seemed to be someone just outside his reach toward which he directed his venom. I was merely a spectator in a one man play that spanned over a full century, four generations, two world wars, one Korean "conflict" and one police action in Viet Nam.

"WHAT THE HELL IS A POLICE ACTION? 60,000 AMERICANS WERE KILLED! DOES THAT SOUND LIKE A POLICE ACTION TO YOU, DAVID?"

There was no halfway point in his Victor's life. He lived to see it all.

To an eighteen year old high school senior who thinks he's got the world by the balls, a man like Mr. Victor Karl seems like a thirty minute sitcom you would watch on Thursday nights. You sit and listen to him for a while, you laugh at the brazen way he looks at things and the crass manner in which he describes his life, and then the show is over. You snicker a little bit to yourself when he farts in the middle of talking. And when he holds the picture with the silver frame in his lap – the one with his three sons in their Class A uniforms before they went off to war –you have to make a conscious effort not to roll your eyes because he's shown you that same picture 30 times already. You smile like you're looking at a child when spittle and remnants of his lunch make their way out of his mouth as he is describing the trees of his youth; trees that are his brothers and sisters. Trees that mirror his age and yet will still outlive him. And in the middle of a story you've heard already, you look at your watch and wonder if he would notice if you just got up and left like you could in the middle of a situational comedy that wasn't that funny…or situational. As the theme music starts to play like an award show that has been running long, you start to get up to gather your things. You say goodbye but he isn't listening.

Then you go home, but Mr. Victor Karl sits alone by the window looking up into the sky at the brewing of the ten thousandth rainstorm that he has seen in his long life. His dark, hazy eyes match the colors of the threatening clouds. He sits still and drifts off into space searching the nooks and crannies of the past century for any memory that will remind him that he was once revered; that he was once respected, loved and sought after for what he could build and repair. He was loved by women and admired by men. As these memories wash over him, he will soar over the years that have long since fallen away. He will visit every shadow of his past looking for elements of his existence as he remembered them, not as they were documented in a photo album that no one looks at anymore or a faded yellow newspaper clipping no one will ever read. Jobs that he was proud of and land that he worked hard to make his own will pass beneath him. He will float toward the fragrances of women that he has long since forgotten. He will hover weightlessly through the sounds made by his sons as they turn a wrench on an old car or hit the sweet spot of a baseball with a little league bat. He will gather up all these treasures and bring them back to a crippled old life in that antiseptic little room with those angels of mercy and the dim lights in the hallway. He will wrap himself in them and pray to no one. He doesn't care about the next morning. He never plans on being there when it begins. But then he does wake up the next morning, he will swear silently as he goes searching all over again.

I've often thought longevity of life would be a curse. I would consider it a punishment from my God. How dare he "bless me" with more years of life than he has blessed others; my son…my daughter…their children, Teresa, etc. We all experience time as it fades in and out of our lives without any real care as to who gets more of it and who gets less, until the time comes when someone doesn't have any left. When I was eighteen years old, I operated under the ridiculous illusion that I had all the time in the world. Even after visits with Victor, I still didn't appreciate the moments that were surrounding me as well as those ahead of me. To me, time was like water from a very, *very* deep well. You always plan on it being in great abundance. You turn the faucet on and the water comes out. Sometimes, for reasons unknown, the water comes out a little slower or tastes a little funnier but it still comes and after a while you just recognize those hiccups of productivity that the well provides. The funny thing about well water is that it isn't always in abundance. Sometimes it goes bad and sometimes it just goes. Victor knew this and despite the fact that he was blessed (or cursed, depending on how you look at it) with over 100 years of life, he knew that it was not only the journey that mattered, but each stop along the way. I often wonder if Victor would have accepted the blessing of a long life had he known that it would have been 100+ years ahead of him culminating in a small cramped room in a cramped nursing home located in a cramped logging town at the base of the Olympic Peninsula in Washington State. I wonder if he would have done things differently in his life if he knew how it would all come to an end. I wonder about that myself, come to think of it.

Victor Karl died the day after I turned 19 years old. He was 106. My mom called me and said she left the room after getting him set up in his chair. He was sitting by the window looking outside like he always used to do. She came back a few minutes later and he had passed. I remember the exact thing I was doing when she called. I was also sitting by a window, eating a cheeseburger and drinking my second beer. I looked down into the bottom of the bottle and wondered what Victor was thinking when the water stopped coming.

I don't know what gifts he was given throughout his long life. But I do know what gifts he gave me. Thank you, Victor, for the lessons of appreciation and patience. I hope wherever this finds you, you have plenty of deep, cool water from which to drink.

Highway Noises

When you can hear the highway from where you sleep, it's time to find a new place to sleep. I have lived in a couple of places like that. My wife has lived in a place like that too, actually. I can put up with it. Lord knows I have slept in worse spots in my life. But I've always thought that Teresa is too good to live in a place where that kind of aggravating din never quite goes away. She dreams to live in a place that has a garden and a yard with a lawn for me to mow as she prunes a rose bush. She will insist on doing the pruning because I won't do it right.

Unfortunately, I have come to understand the sound of a busy highway. For the better part of my adult life, I have tried to move away from the hum of traffic but, ironically, it has become a steady measure of my heartbeat. Highway traffic is a droning hum of rubber on wet pavement. There was a time in my life when I couldn't hear myself think—or I couldn't hear God's voice—without hearing the sound of traffic. That was a problem for me. I couldn't hear the peace that sometimes comes from white noise. All I heard was the whoosh of hurtling metal and an aching hum that never quite left me. I couldn't get that muffled sound out of my head. It reminded me of the jobs that I had to chase in order to pay for a life of decisions I made. The drone of the road tells the story that I am not the father I always wanted to be. It is the background soundtrack to the hours I've spent driving away from my children or taking them away from the home they are comfortable with to spend every other weekend with a man they know on an hourly basis rather than wholly and completely. To me, the vibration of the highway is the byproduct of leaving.

My wife's garden—away from the highway—will be a holy place. It will be a place of serenity and decency. And as with any garden, the fertilizer that makes the best things grow is often comprised of the foulest things imaginable. So, the soil of her garden will be rich from the seepage of worry that leaves her body; originating from her mind, it is pumped like sewage through the valves and arteries of her super-system and exits from the soles of her feet.The ground will consist of apprehension about bills, taxes, jobs, and the overall distresses of who likes us and who doesn't. The gThe ground will be reeking of corruptible, stagnant ooze from her feet as the stress of her human life bleeds from her pores. And once it hits the crumbly black earth, it will soak into ito the soil and become decomposed by the billion-year-old grounddesign. Nothing bad from our bodies will survive in the soil. The soil of her garden will transform those worries into new lifeThe ground of her garden will bring new life to those worries. The pain will transformmorph itself into the best tomatoes: ripe, red, and luscious. God is funny that way. From mortgage payments, to brown dirt, to vitamin C.

I imagine my wife kneeling in the dirt of her gardenShe sits with her knees in front of her, her delicate hands in the earth. Her golden retriever, Pearl, lies on the ground beside her, because wherever Teresa goes, so goes Pearl. Teresa is digging up something. Her eyes are happy. She sings softly to herself and to her constant four-legged companion. This is where her heart is will be renewed. I will watch her from our balcony. She doesn't know I am there. Pearl turns her head at the slightest creak of wood beneath my feet. The dog gets up as if she is going to come greet me, but she can't leave Teresa. So, she stands and stares for a moment, perplexed by which decision to make. Ultimately she stays, circles a few times, and lies back down in the dirt next to her best friend.

Teresa sifts the ground between her fingers. She thinks of her father and the moments spent with him; quiet, simple, and reverent times. She misses him today. Pearl instinctively looks up at her as if to say, "I know." Pearl rises and shuffles over a few steps to smell her face.

Teresa also uses this garden as a time portal. She rewinds back to the moments where she has her children crawling into her lap, or, all at once, standing before her, at all ages and at all times. They laugh as they wrestle with one another and cry as they embrace to form the perfect self-supporting triangle of family. They have and will restore one another. She fast-forwards to the moments with her granddaughter. She sits beside the child who wields a little plastic shovel and a bucket with lady bugs painted on it. The little girl is helping her grandmother dig holes for new tulip bulbs. With little chubby fingers, the child carefully plops a bulb where her grandmother tells her to and looks up for approval as she taps the soil into place with her small hands. Pearl is there, too, and the three of them become the trilogy of happiness for one another.

With these thoughts and this image, Teresa tilts her head toward the soil and peers into the world. The vibrations of the earth's rotation find the humming pitch of her soul. A harmony exists here. This place and this time is where she was created. This moment next to her dog, with the memories of the life she has had and the images of the one to come—along with tomatoes ripening, vegetables at the point of harvest, and the sun on her face—is where life begins (and has always begun) for her.

This is God away from traffic. And this is what I want for my wife.

Only in Pairs

I've recently discovered that when you're laid up with a pretty nasty flu bug, you have the energy to think about things only in pairs. For instance, chicken soup sounds OK; French onion soup, not so much. Saltine crackers aren't bad but Doritos are a poor choice. Club soda is good for the stomach while diet root beer is an accident waiting to happen. In short, you narrow things down to what will not be too unpleasant if, God forbid, you had to experience it a second time. And for the record, if I ever meet the rat bastards who invented fruit-punch-flavored Robitussin, I'm going to punch them in the throat. They're not fooling anyone, you know. We all know it's still Robitussin.

When my temperature rises and my body starts aching, I can muster only two independent thoughts at the same time. For instance, with a 102°F fever and bones feeling like they all had been recently broken and reset, my thoughts turned to the comfort of my bed versus the coolness of the side of the toilet. Also, while standing in the kitchen, I wondered if a glass of water would require a Herculean effort to drink, or whether dehydration has gotten a bum rap. Lastly, while molded to the couch like it was a physical part of my body, I wondered whether I should lie there with my full bladder and hope to die, or make the long arduous trek to the bathroom where I discover I shouldn't have left it in the first place. Everything in pairs. It's in the bible.

When you're healthy, most normal people have a myriad of things pinging around in their brains. There are four projects to do at work, the yard needs to be mowed, the kids have dentist appointments on Saturday right in the middle of the AFC Championship game, and why won't a perfectly healthy dog stop rubbing his ass on the new rug. There's a juggling act involved, and how well you keep the balls in the air is the byproduct of a healthy mind and body. But when your mind and body are under attack, the polarity of what works and what doesn't, the sick and the healthy, the right and wrong, and the easy and hard all come into the forefront of reality. So, as I was smack-dab in the middle of my waltz with Señora Influenza, I decided to list my own pairings that have taken center stage:

- Wine and food: While it's true that some wine varietals reveal their underlying qualities more elegantly when paired with certain foods, it is my humble opinion that wine was never created to be such a bitchy, stick-up-the-butt cultural identifier. For shit's sake. . . it's really just fermented grape juice, after all. If I choose to have red wine with a ham and cheese omelet, or a glass of champagne with my spaghetti and meatballs, then I freaking dare the wine snobs to knock on my door and look down their noses at my culinary decisions. Given the mood in which I find myself, I'd end up smothering them with my daughter's old Dora the Explorer pillow. Fat lot of good it's doing to keep my head from exploding.

- Words and music: Lennon and McCartney. Henley and Frey. Page and Plant. Jagger and Richards. Rogers and Hammerstein. Loggins and Messina. Sometimes the greatest music has come from two minds. And when they put the music on the bars along with the words on the page then you get such amazing pieces of art like "Hotel California" and "When the Levee Breaks." It's hard to even imagine one without the other. Do you think that "Ticket to Ride" would have been the same song had only John Lennon written it? And Keith Richards, no doubt, would have written some good stuff on his own but damned if anyone would have understood what he was saying. Words and music. Separately, neither have to be brilliant to be good. But both have to be together to be brilliant.

- Ali and Frazier: Insert any legendary boxers here. Ali and Foreman. Leonard and Hagler. Hagler and Hearns. It doesn't matter. They all needed each other to establish their legacy. You can pick any sport, for that matter: Yankees and Red Sox. Packers and Vikings. Manchester United and. . . well, that's the only soccer team I've heard of, so let's just go with them. The epic battle between two foes is only truly defined when both rise to the challenge and meet each other at their very best. It got me thinking about men and women. Friends and neighbors. We all remember the greatest elements of our lives but they only truly happen when a defining moment is met by a reciprocating effort. Think of the best moments in your life. More than likely, these moments were created after a series of events or a collection of equally charged efforts all came together at just the right time, ushered in by just the right people under just the right circumstances. In short, you get what you give.

And lastly, the greatest pairing for me is the one that has changed my life forever. I distinctly remember a very early morning on one of the first days of January, 2002. My daughter Morgan was born only a few weeks before and while her mother was getting some well-deserved sleep I was awake with my newborn daughter and my two year old son. We were downstairs together, all sharing space on the couch, while the house remained dark and the fireplace was glowing. Max was cuddled up next to me and nodding off with a sippy cup of juice in his hand while Morgan was asleep in my arms. We were all covered up by a large fleece blanket and the peaceful notes of Bach's Cello Suite No. 1 was floating through the cozy stillness from the stereo in the den.

I looked down at my children and realized that my soul was taking shape; it was edging toward completion. For years, I had a huge emptiness inside of me that no amount of alcohol, fighting, travel, or running away could fill. It was an abysmal way to learn of life's riches and disappointments. But when I held those two lives in the quiet of my home, I felt an emotional coupling that only occurs when a father holds his children. To suggest that—in those wee hours of the morning—my children and I "bonded" would be a massive understatement. It was truly a heavenly connection that, I believe, we are all meant to experience at least once in our lives. As I held my two children and felt the pairing of our hearts, my lifelong desire to be at peace with the world around me and my wish to recognize an earthly purpose for myself became a bit more clear. I may not be—in the most traditional sense—the full-time dad that you see on TV or in the movies. I may not be there every moment of their young lives to ensure they get their homework done, learn how to change tires, or listen to questions about how crazy girls are or how mean boys can be. But I know some full-time dads who aren't me, either. I'll drive four hundred miles to spend an afternoon with them when other dads won't cross the room for their kids. I'll learn to cook something healthy rather than have them remember only pizza boxes and paper sack dinners while at Dad's house. And I will answer painful questions as honestly as I can, even if it paints an unflattering picture of their old man. There are many paths to understanding and sometimes the ugly truth is one of those paths.

As I look to the duality of things I'm reminded of a passage I read years ago, from Robert Fulghum. "I believe that imagination is stronger than knowledge. That myth is more potent than history. That dreams are more powerful than facts. That hope always triumphs over experience. That laughter is the only cure for grief. And I believe that love is stronger than death." In the simplest of terms, Fulghum found a way to illuminate that life, happiness, and health all reside with the grasp of the light and dark, the yin and the yang, the up and the down, in sickness and in health, for richer or poorer and till death do us part.

Him and her. Them and me. You and I. Somehow I find comfort in those pairs, regardless how I'm feeling at the moment.

Rocket Man

The tunnel was cold and damp, like any good tunnel should be. At the entrance—on that dividing line between daylight and dark—stood thousands of hysterical onlookers. They were climbing over one another to get a peek into the blackness from which he would emerge. He could hear their frantic cheers and rhythmic chants. They had waited all morning for his arrival. He had waited his whole life for this moment.

Astride his trusted machine, he could hear his own heartbeat reverberate within his chest and up through his throat. Its steady pulse thumped like a bass drum while his raspy, nervous exhales kept perfect time with the downbeat of his heart. His breath echoed in the chamber of his helmet. He closed his eyes and pictured exploding out of the darkness of the tunnel into the bright morning sky.

The schedule of the jump kept changing. He wanted the conditions to be perfect. Once decided upon, his handlers spread the word like wildfire. He originally wanted an evening jump, under the bright street lights. He dreamt of screaming out of the unknown blackness, flying down the alley of people that came thousands of miles to see him, and rocket up the ramp toward the heavens. He wanted to fly through the night like he was created to do. But he had to be in bed by seven o'clock.

"What is he doing?" The hardened man sidled up next to his petite wife, who was looking out of the dirty living room window at their son. She was still in her nursing scrubs after just arriving home from a long, overnight shift at the nursing home. He was sipping on a grungy cup of coffee, discolored from constant use since 1971. That cup hadn't been in contact with dish soap since its creation.

She answered without looking at him. "Hell if I know." She shrugged. "He's been sitting on his bike staring down the street for about ten minutes now."

The father looked down the street about fifty yards to a makeshift ramp built from a rotting sheet of plywood propped up by an old metal toolbox. He recognized the tool box immediately as the one that took up center station on the counter in his garage. "Oh, hell if he is!" he said sharply. He put the cup down on the end table next to the ashtray and strode toward the front door.

In one half of the daredevil's mind, a clock counted down. Every downtick of the seconds was an upsurge of energy. In the other half of his mind, he prayed. He prayed the mechanics had done their job and the ramp technicians theirs. He prayed the wind would calm at the moment he launched into the air. He prayed that his two wheeled rocket would give him one more soft landing. He prayed that Cindy Shell was in the crowd and that she was wearing her baton-twirling outfit. He imagined himself as a little boy, alone in the vast expanse of a hollow mountain; a single beam of light boring down from the peak thousands of feet above his head. The beam found him on his knees. His lips moved silently as he prayed for the success of his mission. He prayed for his family: that they would remain healthy, even though he didn't really mean it. He prayed that he would be recognized rather than reproached. He prayed that—when he flew through the air—he would keep flying; away from all the infected streets and eggshell houses in all the dirty towns, and away from the hurtful people who paid their hard-earned whiskey money to watch him crash and die. He prayed that he would land safely and—at the same time—not land at all. The paradox of his life was within sight, just on the other side of the plastic shield of his helmet.

He counted down the final seconds in his mind and—right before zero—he made a cross on his chest, although he wasn't sure why since he didn't really know what that meant. He jolted his machine in gear and peeled out from the soft gravel onto the hardness of the pavement. He was barreling toward his destiny, in full view of those souls who had nowhere else to go.

The old man stepped off the concrete porch and into the front yard. As he angrily lit another cigarette he made a beeline for the street where his son was now pedaling madly toward the ramp. "Hey!" he bellowed. He put two fingers to his mouth and whistled loudly. It was a piercing indicator that meant so many things: dinner was on the table, it's time to come home, or you're one step away from being murdered. From city blocks away, once that whistle hit the airwaves, its intended recipients had a very finite amount of time to come to attention or suffer the consequences of having to be sought after and dragged home by the scruff of the neck.

      The boy on the bike didn't appear to hear the man. He was laser-focused to a point past the ramp, farther down the street, possibly as far as the next block. For a moment, the old man didn't think the boy was heading toward the plywood being held upright by his most treasured possession. Perhaps he wouldn't have to hit the kid after all. But just when he thought that the boy had heard his whistle and was pedaling toward some other target, the kid turned the bike toward the groove in the ramp and pumped his legs maniacally, his arms pulling the bike from side to side but his head remaining steady as the center of gravity.

    "HEY! GODDAMN IT! COME HERE, NOW!"

    The six neighborhood street rats who had gathered to watch the crazy kid jump his raggedy Huffy bike five feet into the air now embarrassingly turned their attention to the old man who was half-running, half-limping, toward the boy. He would never make it in time. He was a thousand years too late.

    The machine hummed at a high pitch, full throttle at maximum output. It couldn't go any faster. It didn't need to. All he heard was his heartbeat and the whooshing of the wind in his ears. It was the one thing he didn't factor into his pre-jump calculations. He could manage the crosswind in flight as he didn't have a landing ramp to accommodate for. It was the headwind that worried him. *Too late now*, he thought. He was at the doorstep of history.

    He saw his chief mechanic running toward him, frantically waving his arms and shouting something incoherent. He was too fixated to consider what could possibly be the matter at that point. The mechanic was always trying to get him to abort his jumps. He was overly cautious about everything. He was too inflexible. He had no vision. And he smoked too much and drank in the morning, which made him unreliable, unreasonable, and unpredictable for the rest of the day. In the briefest of seconds, he made a mental note to fire the mechanic the moment he landed.

All the earthly elements blurred in his mind to become one single point of light that illuminated the bottom of the ramp. The sides of the street and the onlookers become one and the same. The trees grew instantaneously, blocking out the sun, and then became fixed as if in a painting. He held his breath. His destiny was now only a few feet away.

He hit the ramp at an alarming speed. The world froze in that moment. The stability beneath him evaporated. He was no longer tied to the earth. He was not a man. There was no machine beneath him. He was a part of the sky. The past and present melted away, becoming a steady, inviting glow of things unknown. For a nanosecond, he closed his eyes and whispered one last thought to the universe.

"Tomorrow."

He knew that crying never worked on his parents like it worked for Ricky Gayle, the little scraggly kid that lived at the end of a one lane half dirt, half paved road that emptied into the parking lot of an abandoned gravel pit. Ricky could get away with anything. One time he got caught stealing caramels out of the bulk section of the Red Apple grocery store. The assistant manager walked Ricky all the way home so he could confess his crime to his own mother. Ricky whipped up a face full of tears two minutes before entering the front door and just like that, she melted and ended up scolding the assistant manager for embarrassing her son in front of his friends. So, when the daredevil came to his senses after what amounted to be a spectacular crash, resulting in a bent bicycle frame, cracked handle bars, and a gash in his knee the size of a silver dollar, he quickly knew that whatever excuse he had to come up with could not involve sobbing for mercy. He thought about running away from home but realized he wouldn't get far on a broken Huffy.

He heard the jingling of his father's key chain coming down the street. He thought he heard the man cursing under his breath. He half expected to hear the clearing of a leather belt through pant loops. The boy could almost smell his father approaching; it was an ever-present odor that constantly hovered in the rooms that housed nearly all of the boy's worst memories. It was an odiferous cocktail made up of sweat, cigarette smoke, and freshly cut lumber. The injured boy closed his eyes and waited for the inevitable cuffing upside the head. By now, he was use to the shock. He just hoped his friends weren't there to see it.

The old man kneeled down to pull the bike off of the fallen hero. He put his large hand on his son's chest to force him to lay back down and then brushed the dirt from the boy's face. The boy flinched at first, but then painfully succumbed to the extremely rare, tender moment that was unfolding before him. With a gentleness the child never saw before, the man rolled up the shredded pant leg of his son's blue jeans in order to survey the injury. He blew a soft, low whistle as he gently picked and brushed away little pieces of rock and dirt from the deep cut on his son's knee.

Without saying another word the man scooped up the boy and carried him back to the house where his mother was waiting for him with a washcloth and hydrogen peroxide. It was ten minutes past seven on Saturday night.

Sandwiches

The other morning, I woke up with a better than average feeling in my head and chest. The room, normally darkened by the shade and the grayness of an autumn dawn in the Pacific Northwest, was bright and inviting. I cleared my eyes with the back of my hand and looked across to the only window in my studio apartment. The morning's first light came seeping in through the velour blinds. The sunshine I had hoped for finally arrived. I didn't want to have to trudge through the streets of Portland with Max in low spirits because of cold November rains.

After a morning of short errands and fidgeting around the cramped space of my studio until the agreed upon time finally arrived, it became time to text my son:

Ready?

After a few minutes, the soft ping from my phone issued his reply:

OH YEA!

Our mission was a television reality show sandwich that would simply blow our minds. I had seen all of the episodes on the Food Network about the hole in the wall burger, pizza and sandwich joints. I wanted to finally stop talking about "we should" and file it under "done." So, this weekend was going to be epic. We were to find the best sandwich spot in all of Portland, Oregon. That was my goal. Actually, that was Max's goal. My goal was to muscle in as much time as I could with my boy who was becoming a man right before my eyes.

Max was waiting on his porch with a hooded sweatshirt and his hair fixed "just so." Rolling up to the driveway, I powered down the window and in my best bass voice offered up the invitation to gluttony.

"Hey, bub. You ready to indulge?"

He bounded down the stairs and did a Dukes of Hazard hood slide across the front of my car. He over juiced his jump and nearly wiped out in the rose bushes. Giggling, he threw open the door and fell into the copilot's seat.

The sandwich spot was in North Portland. I had to parallel park a few blocks away in a cramped little space that was sure to piss of the people that were on either side of me. I didn't give a crap. I was with my boy. These moments don't come around as often as I'd like. We tried to dodge the heavy pelts of rain as we scooted down the sidewalk toward the corner café with an open street front entrance. The menu was a giant chalkboard on the wall. The ingredients were all out in the open and the grill was a few feet in front of our faces. Total sandwich transparency. We were doing it.

It turns out that the sandwiches weren't that bad. They weren't mind blowing, but they were better than what I could have done which is generally my barometer when it comes to paying for a meal. Max had a turkey on whole grain with cranberry dressing and aioli spread. I had a chicken pesto on a freshly made French roll. They were good. Not what we expected, but the conversation was fun and the atmosphere was cool. As we drove home, we decided that we should go to a place I had heard about in the state capital which was 45 minutes away. One day…we would.

That night, I dreamt of my father. I actually wondered in my dream if he ever thought of doing things like taking his son out to a hole in the wall diner to see if the "best cheeseburger in town" turned out to be really the best or if it was no better than a McDonald's quarter pounder. I remember him bringing home food from the local tavern and occasionally the fast food place that he liked on the other side of town, but it was more of a "feed the family" thing rather than sharing time together. I don't blame him for not doing that kind of stuff. The man wasn't wired that way. He was a "cause and effect" type of guy; you did something and then, as a result of that action, something happened. He bought food so his kids wouldn't starve. What he wouldn't do was drive 100 miles for a sandwich, no matter what kind of bread they used.

I also dreamt of my daughter, Morgan, who likes sandwiches too, but what she craves is dessert. I dreamt she and I would go to the most famous bakery in Paris and while we were waiting for freshly made chocolate silk pie she would sing her soul wringing version of Ave Maria. People gathered around the bakery to hear her sing and she became embarrassed so she stopped. The echo of her voice was still drifting through the room when I woke up at three in the morning. I wiped the tears away from my face as I lay in bed and listened to the rain pelt the window of my apartment. The lingering melody of Ave Maria and the image of my daughter holding the final note among her small audience cut through the fog of my subconscious. I laid awake for two hours thinking of chocolate silk pies and the power of daughters.

      A few weekends later, Max and I would finally get to that little place in the state capital and discover that it wasn't bad, but the avocado would be slightly brown and the "just baked" olive loaf wouldn't really be just baked, so we would look online while in the car and see that a hole in the wall place in Central Oregon was once on TV for having amazing prime rib roasted sandwiches. We would plan on driving four hours to Sisters, Oregon.

      When we would eventually get to Sisters, we found out that it was not such a bad sandwich. I had the prime rib dip which was advertised as the "Best in the State of Oregon" and Max would resort back to his childhood appetites of a grilled cheese with a cup of tomato soup but this time it would have a little twist; melted Gouda on rye with a bowl of lobster bisque. We would share a homemade kosher dill pickle. It was a good lunch. We would both agree that even the fresh lemonade was worth the trip.

      Max and I talked about cars on the way home. We talked about how he liked basketball but knew that he'd never be all that good at it. I would tell him I was the exact same, except for the part about liking basketball. I talked about the jobs I've held. Max wouldn't initially understand my desire (a grown up's desire) to work for a paycheck rather doing something that you love. I told him that often times, unfortunately, grown ups end up doing things not because they stimulate us and fuel our passions, but because they comfortably pay the bills. And once the bills are paid, we hold out hope that we will eventually save enough to pursue other things.

      "Why don't you start off with the 'other things' and that way you take out the temptation to pursue something else." he asked.

"Damn good question, son, and a good point. I suppose it depends on what the other things are and how well they take care of you and who you love." It was all I could come up with in terms of an answer. I didn't have the heart to tell him I've been asking myself that same question for almost 40 years. I was torn between hoping he would never understand that frustrating dichotomy thus always choosing to do something he loved, and making sure he had enough money in the bank to buy shelter, medicine, and sandwiches.

We drove in silence for a while.

"Somewhere along the way, the road seems to change on you, Max. Sometimes you don't even know that your priorities have changed until you're good and lost and then when look around and don't recognize a damn thing—yourself or anything else—then you start reaching for those 'other things' to make sure you stay afloat in life." I was saying it more to myself and the hum of the car's heater then anyone else. "You just make a choice while on one of those roads and then you keep going."

"Wow, Dad…" he said. "That's deep." He smiled at me like he just got away with something, then he cranked up the volume on the car radio. "Let's stop and get a latte or something" he shouted above the music.

A few weeks later we read about a shop in Seattle that makes all of its sandwiches using waffles for the bread, so we took the train to Seattle. We talked about his sister / my daughter. We talked about my divorce from his mother. We talked about women and girls.

We talked about Spain and Greece and Italy and Alaska and Iowa and Montana and Hawaii and all the other places where I've been, worked and played a little too hard. He talked about Cleveland and Nashville and Austin City Limits. He told me about Eddie's Attic in Georgia, Chicago's House of Blues, and The Mississippi Delta. He was surprised I had heard of these places. I quietly reminded him my life did not begin the day he was born (although sometimes I, myself, think it did). He told me about all the places he wants to see. He talked about China andThailand and the Mariana Trench and the temperature change between the sunlight and the shade on the dark side of the moon. The chasm between how he got from

Austin, Texas to the Mariana Trench is expansive, to be sure, but when you're with Max you just roll with it. He builds bridges quickly so you better be ready to cross them.

Iowa and the moon. Greece and Portland. The blues, Texas, Graceland and the Mariana Trench; all via the Amtrak #506 on the Cascade line, Portland to Seattle.

When we pulled into Kings Street Station in Seattle, we took a cab to the piers on the waterfront. To get things started, we walked up to Pikes Place Market and shoved some gum on the wall. Max listenend intently to some street musicians while I ordered a couple of nice chinook filets at the fish market to take home with us. We sampled the ghost pepper jelly and took pictures of ourselves in front of a guy balancing five full fish bowls on his face. Then, we hailed another cab and asked them to take us to Lake Union and Duke's Chowder House. Max and I heard that Duke's had a fresh salmon salad served on an open face lemon crescent, so Max ordered that and I had a bowl of their Dungeness Crab and Bourbon Chowder with a small round of roasted garlic focaccia to sap up what my spoon couldn't capture. I looked across the table at my son and told him that I loved him. He nodded back at me and mumbled through a mouthful of sandwich, "Mmmm hmmm. Paging Doctor Cheese. Doctor Cheese, please report to table number twenty-two."

On the night train home, as the railcar was dimmed and the other passengers were resting or quietly listening to their own music, Max looked out the window to the darkness that veiled the countryside whizzing by. I looked at him and wondered if he thought this day was as brilliant to him as it had been to me. I wondered if he knew that any moment spent together was a moment that repairs my cellular structure; it makes me stronger and allows me to breathe more deeply. I wondered if he galvanized those seconds in time as dutifully as I did. I wondered if he knew that these kind of days were becoming rarer as the years drifted on. He caught me staring at him. He grinned and gave me a thumbs up sign. Upon which another hour passed as we became hypnotized by the clicking of the rails.

Suddenly, without notice, he leaned into me and whispered, "I heard about this place in New York City that is like a hundred years old or something and they are supposed to have the best brisket po'boys in the world. I've never had one of those. Are they good?" I nodded back and him and said, "Damn good." He turned back to the window and smiled to himself.

So, we would decide to go New York City someday.

You know…just for the sandwiches.

Happy Birthday to Me

    I don't remember too many birthdays I've had over the years. I remember my twelfth. My mom threw me a birthday party and several of my neighborhood and grade-school friends showed up. A few of us stayed up very late, eating three tons of the newly discovered Cool Ranch Doritos and drinking a bathtub-full of Mountain Dew. Only two of my friends stayed over. The rest of them didn't like the accommodations, and came down with immediate cases of gastric distress. I don't blame them for bailing on the party. There were hundreds of nights I wanted to run away from that place myself. But I suppose it could have *actually* been gastric distress. Try eating nothing but Doritos and drinking Mountain Dew for four hours and see if your bowels aren't doing the Macarena.

    I spent nearly every waking hour of the day I turned sixteen driving around in my dad's big brown Ford truck. I had just gotten my driver's license and damned if I wasn't going to wring every second out of that day, taking advantage of my newly acquired freedom. Dad's Ford was a beast: huge tires, four-wheel drive, eight-track tape player, and three—count 'em . . . THREE!—tanks of gas. The truck came with a front and rear tank and Dad added a fifty-five-gallon tank in the back. All three tanks were full, and so I packed a grungy nylon duffle bag with books, four baloney sandwiches, a plastic milk jug full of water, a thermos of hot chocolate, a few handheld video games, a spiral notebook, four pencils, a pocketknife and a bunch of eight-track tapes of bands that I couldn't get enough of: Supertramp, Grand Funk Railroad, Rush, The Allman Brothers, Eric Clapton with Derrick and The Dominos, Three Dog Night, Creedence Clearwater Revival, and for some reason . . . Carly Simon. I didn't really care much about Carly Simon's music, so I expect my appreciation was for her album covers. I fell in love her long before she told me "You're So Vain."

    I drove for hours around the city that I grew up in and along the country roads that surrounded it. As much as I thought I knew that mossy little timber town, I found myself going places that were completely foreign to me. I found side streets that emptied into little neighborhood parks that I didn't know existed. I ventured up steep, winding logging roads (probably on private property) as I climbed deep into the hills of Mason County. I drove along a curving two-lane highway that borders the emerald-green waters of Hood Canal and made my way up to mountain lakes and into a rainforest on the Olympic Peninsula of Washington State. The excitement I felt by being unrestricted was sprinkled generously with a nervousness of being alone on the open road. That birthday trip was the kernel that would take root deep within the soil of my soul, as I would spend the next thirty years of my life feeling more at peace on the open road and alone than I ever did in the company of friends and family. Only my children and my wife give me that same sense of belonging and serenity.

My twenty-first birthday passed in Bellingham, Washington, while I was attending Western Washington University. This memorable milestone of the legality of adulthood started off with me proudly walking into the corner market to *legally* buy my first six-pack of beer. Up until that point, I'd had an identification card that not so cleverly (and quite phonily) identified me as "Hector Hollings," born in 1960 (I was actually born in 1967), all of six feet, two inches (I'm a scosh over five feet ten) and a slightly balding red head (at the time, I had a full head of brown hair). In a brilliant display of idiocy, I stood in front of the same guy I'd been buying my Mickey's Big Mouths from for the past year and was actually dumb enough to proudly show him my real ID. He looked at it, looked back at me, and said, "Hmmm . . . you're not Hector anymore?" He promptly sold me my beer and told me to never come back.

My thirtieth was the only surprise birthday party I've ever had in my life, and my fortieth birthday was spent in the company of a few close friends, loving, laughing, and feeling that all is right with the world.

At the time of this writing, I'm knocking on the door of my fiftieth birthday. I've often heard people say that turning a year older means very little to them. They'll rattle off lines like "It's just a number" or "It's just another day" as they accept well wishes, have a little cake, or unwrap the ugliest tie ever purchased at Walmart. Then, toward the end of the evening, they settle into their beds with perhaps some notion of setting new goals to encourage them toward another twelve months of survival upon this mortal coil. There is absolutely nothing wrong with celebrating this way, I suppose. Whatever floats one's boat is generally okay with me, but I just never thought this kind of pedestrian existence would appeal to me. But the older I get the more I realize that full throttle exhilaration and a reckless pursuit of happiness is taking a back seat to soulful introspection and the quiet hum of peace and harmony.

So, with this easier perspective in mind—and while I'm standing on the doorstep of (hopefully) another half century on this planet—I'm going to take a different turn on the same old goals I've made in the past.

Goal #1: I plan on loving my kids even more in the coming year despite their fading out of my memory as "children" and growing into their adulthood. I may not be there every day. I may not see their daily development or pick up on all of their ever increasing quirks of personality. I may even miss some of those milestones like prom night, driving tests, or their first heartbreak. But in the moments that I have them in my life. . . in those days that I am happily ensconced in their attention and love. . . they will have every ounce of my heart. I will take long walks with them and listen to their stories about their daily routines and the people they meet. I will sit with them over meals and laugh with them as they quote lines from their favorite episodes of Spongebob Squarepants. I will hear them play their latest piece on the guitar or watch them rehearse their lines for a play. I'll beam with pride at the work they've put in to their passions and compliment them on their efforts. My influence on the details of their day to day lives may fade away, but it will be replaced by a recognition of their own energies and passions. And my love will evolve from the constant attention to their safety to an appreciation of their lives as they become healthy and happy humans.

Goal #2: In the past, my body has treated me rather poorly. To put a more blunt point on it, it's crapped out entirely. I can't say that I blame it. The closest I've come to treating this shell as a temple involved stumbling past churches in Portland during the annual Pub Crawl for Charity. In my newest year, I will work toward a healthier existence. Meaning no disrespect to the newly dependent world of "better body by chemistry," I will get back to the basics; avoid a sedentary existence, put my body in motion, eat less, inhale deeply, exhale calmly. I will take long rides on the bike and seek out steeper terrain on unknown trails. I will recreate benchmarks on fitness as a man in his fifties; three hour weight room sessions at the gym will be replaced by laps at the pool and even a kickboxing class or two. It might be nice to fight for health reasons rather than self defense. In short, I will focus more on my physical core. I will also graft into my daily routine exercises that will nurture my mind. I will read more, write more, and rediscover a confidence in my communication and creativity that existed a long time ago but had since gotten lost in the jungle of my own self-doubt. My strength will start from the inside and work its way out. You'll see it in my eyes and my face first, and my ass will bring up the rear.

Goal #3: God and I have been passing each other in the halls of my life of late, with me nodding indifferently like one would nod at a coworker one doesn't really know (but pretends to) while on the way to one's cubicle. Although daily prayer has always been a staple for me, I fear I've been asking not to lose anything in my life rather than praying for something miraculous to happen. In short, I've been walking on eggshells with the Almighty. Generally, I'm thinking that is not the design He had in mind for me. So, I will spend some time understanding those blueprints a bit more. I will see how I can help the people around me. I will go out of my way—and out of my comfort zone—to make someone's path a little easier or to show others that basic human decency and compassion still exist. I will take more time for coffee visits and phone calls with those around me that may be starving for just someone to talk to. In short, I will look *out* so as to help me look *up* in order to know more about my Creator. Because, in the echoing brilliance of C.S. Lewis, "God cannot give us a happiness and peace apart from himself, because it is not there. There is no such thing."

Goal #4: On the same thread as the previous goal, I will repair my friendships and attempt to create new ones. In the not-so-distant past, I've fooled myself into thinking that taking a violent turn toward independence is the only way to overcome the slings and arrows of outrageous fortune. Logically, this makes as much sense as sandpapering a wildcat's ass in a phone booth, but when you're locked into your own bubble of self-righteousness and depravity, logic and reason sometimes take a back seat to pigheadedness. I say "sometimes" because if you don't have great friends—true friends—you can fool yourself into believing you're on your own. I've recently looked around and realized that those whom I call friends have not only never left my side but have stood in the path of those arrows that were hell-bent on killing my mind, body and soul. While it's true that I have lost some friends as a result of my egotism, I'll be damned if I'm going to lose any more. So, while I will reach out to repair old bonds and look to say "hello" to some new faces.

I don't know if these goals will ever result in positive outcomes. Sometimes I think that the mere fact they made it onto paper is a good start. I think on them from time to time which allows me to keep them on the front burner of my mind rather than stuffed in the back of my crowded refrigerated brain behind the moldy ideas of community service and an expired carton of losing thirty pounds.

I like my birthday goals. The day I stop creating them is the day I stop having birthdays. At which point, I'm sure I'll have much more serious things to consider.

The Very Private, Super Secret Life of Bert Lavarr

The next few minutes were the most inconvenient and uncomfortable ones of his life. She came in and out of focus a dozen times. Each time gave him a thrill, a sudden jolt of surface energy and—at the same time when she turned toward him—a skin-crawling sensation of shame and discomfort.

His life up to that point had been pleasing enough. Nothing extraordinary had ever happened and that was exactly how he liked it. So, in this same coffee shop, quietly entrenched within the same routine, on the same day that he'd been living for the entirety of his very ordinary life, she appeared out of nowhere. It was an excruciating moment that he never expected.

Normally, he rarely looked up from his plate of two strips of bacon, one over-easy egg, and one slice of dry white toast. To the left of his meal, in a small disheveled space, he penciled in a small journal with a frayed, cracked, leather binding and ripped pages. In the middle of sloppy bites of breakfast that would never quite make it entirely into his mouth, an impulse would surge through him and he'd scribble furiously on the pages, the fork still in his left hand and the stub of a pencil in his right. His elbow dipped into the eggs as he reached across his plate to scribble down an impulsive thought into the journal. And then, as if a peaceful ghost slowly drifted into his earhole and took over his body, he would stop the frantic scribbling and calmly pencil out the stillness of his mind on a clear line. So when he first saw her walk into the diner for the first time he knew she was the embodiment of what he had been writing about for years. He would watch her each time she came into the diner. She never sat anywhere, but always placed the same to-go order; a small, extra hot mocha with a blueberry muffin. He started to capture the moments and restrain them with words, images, and structure. Each time he saw her was like the seconds after a huge explosion, when the sounds of the world get drowned out by a humming, high-pitched tone. He stared for minutes on end at nothing until the hollow noises of the diner returned.

He was a mad, unkempt sort of fellow, a walking human wrinkle ornamented in mismatched clothes, unruly salt-and-pepper hair, and sheets of scratch paper sticking out from every pocket. No one dared sit next to him or even make his acquaintance. His solidarity allowed him to stake a claim to his table—and even the adjoining ones—without worrying about being flanked by other patrons. And should additional ideas warrant more scribbling, more notes, and the layout of a timeline of thoughts, he would dash them down on hastily produced sheets of any type of parchment within reach, like he was trying to freeze in time the last moments of his life.

The diner's lone waitress, Vivian (her nametag simple labeled her as "Viv"), was generally the man's only company at that hour. She was the quintessential truck-stop dive-bar slopper of ham and eggs; curvy figure, long, coiled, dark hair tied up in eleven different places to keep it out of the patrons' food, and brash enough to stand up to the truckers and transients that stumbled into the place. Despite having no formal education past tenth grade, she had an extremely sharp mind and an exhaustive wit. Patrons thought it was some sort of gimmick when she called out to a stranger who had just come in, "You look an eggs Benedict type of guy," and that is what they would order. Most of it was a lucky guess, but she did have a mind to read people and once they ordered, she could mentally catalogue exactly what they had, what they didn't have the stomach for, and when they needed to be left the hell alone.

She knew after this curious little man's first visit that he needed his coffee to stay hot with three quick refills at quarter cup intervals. She stopped wondering about him after the first week of his arrival. She was friendly enough at first. She tried to make small talk by discussing the old standbys: the weather, the condition of the neighborhood, and the city's only professional sports team. When that didn't work, she asked about what he was writing. When she got nothing in return but shrugs and mumbles, she stopped trying. She didn't know why she did it in the first place. She didn't really care to know anything about the guy.

Five months later, she fell into her own routine with him: quiet service (dead silence sometimes) with no questions and no small talk. She placed the order for his breakfast when she saw his bus approaching. The crosstown number eleven. Five-thirty sharp. He paid cash each time and tipped extremely generously. She didn't even know his name.

It wasn't that this rumpled patron of Viv's Diner was an overly obsessive duck by nature. He could have done things differently, he supposed. Why shouldn't he have things the way he wrote about them? Once, he contemplated how this life would look. Over the span of a few morning breakfast sessions at the diner, he wrote a story about a man he wished he would transform into; a man in fresh, clean clothes going to a job that he enjoyed, one that he would keep going to even if they didn't pay him. And then, at the end of the day, this man in fresh, clean clothes would drive home from work in an old, clean pickup truck and feel light and free. On his way home, he would stop into shops, buy organic vegetables and fresh-cut flowers and not worry about whether he could afford them. He would get to his quiet, comfortable home and present his gifts to his wife who would smile back warmly at him and glow from the generousity of these simple gestures.

This fictional man's house was surrounded by eleven clear acres where three fat, slow cows grazed in the back corner of the pasture away from the road. He would have some chickens in a small red shed next to a slightly larger barn where he kept a small tractor, hay for the cows, and the frame of an old car with no wheels. The man even grew grape vines along the back fence of his property and had a go at making his own wine from time to time. The man would teach himself the guitar and play simple songs to his wife in the evenings. He would cook the meals for both of them and feel generally happy that he was alive, dry, and in control of his days.

It was a flowery little piece of writing that even the frumpy writer in the diner didn't fully understand. He wrote about this distorted vision of himself and the simple pleasures of being a quiet, handsome, mysterious man; a man whom other people loved and could trust to get the job done. He wrote about the things this man created and raised on his hobby farm and the work he did for his local community. The small-town women secretly loved this man and the men respected him immensely. And then, during a bad morning at the diner when Vivian was out sick and her replacement was overly chatty and burnt his toast, the frumpy diner writer changed the story dramatically and wrote about how this simple farmer's wife had suddenly died after nearly forty years of marriage. It was a sudden illness that took her quickly, without any explanation as to how or why it happened.

At the small table in the dirty diner, the writer created a grief that nearly destroyed the handsome gentleman farmer. But as a way to cope with the darkness the farmer was slipping into, the disheveled author wrote that the farmer began writing and sending letters to his dead wife, just like he did when they were grade-schoolers together. He wrote that as a young boy of twelve, the farmer would sneak out of his bedroom window, run down a long dark country road and up an even longer, darker country driveway, and slip a note under the girl's front doormat. That routine started a long love affair that included a shy prom request, the first kisses of both of their lives, long walks down dusty roads, a marriage proposal along a slow flowing mountain creek and finally a wedding under the shadows of towering, hundred-year-old pine trees. After thirty-eight years of a deeply faithful and sweetly respectful union, the farmer buried his wife on the land they had bought together.

After her death, the letters the farmer wrote began to have a cathartic effect on him, grounding him to the reality of his loss and bleeding the sadness from his calloused hands. He told her that he had cleaned out the shed that morning and even found time to restack the woodpile. He told her about the weather and that he was expecting snow later in the week, so he promised to get her heavy coat down from the attic and make sure the fireplace was cleaned. He penned simple words of appreciation for the things she used to do for him. "I liked when you had my thermos full in the morning," or, "You always dried out my boots for me when I forgot to put them by the heater." He wrote to her about whom he saw in town that day. He wouldn't dwell on the specifics "because I know you don't like gossip, my love." He wrote who brought plates of food for him and who offered condolences and who offered to "just talk," should he ever need it. He joked with her that it was never the men that made the request to "just talk" and—should his wife not come to him in his dreams like she had done every night since she died—that perhaps he would take up ol' Gladys Carbuncle's offer to "fix him a hot meal some evening." The voice in the letters began to drift more toward the past tense, yet always sprinkled with a hope that somehow she wasn't gone for good. The farmer would end the letters with a few sentences about how much he missed her and that he was looking forward to seeing her again soon, "but not too soon."

The farmer even went so far as to put the letters in envelopes, stick a stamp on the outside, and shove them in the mailbox on his way to work each morning. Eleanor, Route 12's postal carrier, would pick up these letters and when she saw they were to the man's deceased wife with no actual physical address she would cry softly, for she had known the woman well and mourned her death like the rest of the town. Eleanor kept the letters unopened and safe, tucked away in a locked trunk in her sewing room.

After two years and hundreds of letters that were sent but never mailed, the farmer finally made his way back into the community. He volunteered at the local hospital to hold newborns in the nursery. He visited old friends again and offered to help with simple house repairs. He could be seen at the local flea market almost every Saturday browsing the tables and shaking hands with old friends. He started going back to church every Sunday morning and occasionally played in the worship band using the only three chords he knew on the guitar. After another year, the farmer retired from his simple job, went home that very same evening after stopping at the market to pick up some fresh flowers for his wife's gravesite, and fell asleep at a reasonable hour after making himself a piece of barbecue chicken and cucumber salad. It was the last night of his mortal life.

He was buried in his work clothes on the back corner of his property next to his wife; they both were laid to rest under an old Western Red Cedar. Eleanor, the silent recipient of the farmer's letters, never did tell anyone about them. But after the man died, she opened a few to read the words he wrote. She was so taken by them that she finally shared the letters with her husband, who was the editor of the local paper. Her husband sat aghast as he read some of the most poignant, heart-wrenching sentiments he had ever come across in his life. He recrafted the letters into fictional stories and published them under an anonymous name in a backwater weekly newspaper. Soon, the whole community waited anxiously for each edition, never suspecting that this local farmer's grief was tending the soil of their emotional lives.

The simple little man in the diner wrote this forty-thousand word novella about the farmer, his wife, the letters, and the newspaper editor in three days. And when the diner patron fell under the influence of too much Single Malt Lagavulin one night while sitting alone in his cramped apartment, he felt the connection to this widowed farmer so acutely that he physically experienced a painful longing for a normal life like that of his fictional gentleman farmer. In his quiet inebriation, the author felt his own words vibrate in his heart as they became an identify he yearned for rather than the lonely one he was currently living. In a writer's internet chat room, he posted the entire piece online under the pseudonym "Bert Lavarr," hoping no one would notice. Over the next few days, however, people did notice. The chat room was flooded with requests to post more. He was immediately embarrassed by the attention and somewhat ashamed of the weakness within him.

Some local bookworms made a fuss about the story when they read it online and publically called upon the mysterious Bert Lavarr to show up to cafés and bookstores so he could expand on the widowed farmer's story and to even read a few chapters of what he wrote (specifically, some of the letters the farmer penned to his dead wife). The bookworms wanted him to describe how he was able to create deep emotional turbulence in their otherwise boring, mundane lives. The chat room chatters wanted to look into the eyes and at the mind and shake the hand that authored every single piece of hungry, simple passion they had misplaced or never had in the first place. How could the stagnant, still waters of their lives suddenly have noticeable ripples of surface currents, waves longing to pulsate outward in search of adventure, and relationships, and rocks to break against? Even male readers found the piece to be inspiring yet heart-wrenching, but not in the Nicholas Sparks, predictable, overtly sickening sort of way. Within the character created by Bert Lavarr, the male readers found a raw edge along with a common decency. The widowed farmer reminded them of their calling as men: the hard, dedicated line coupled with a soft, respectful delivery. Clint Eastwood meets James Taylor. A warrior poet cloaked as a Marine Corps general.

The simple chat room novella made all of its readers recognize that their life had been cookie-cutter cheese-fests. Bert Lavarr created an alternative to the acceptance of grief in all its forms. Bert Lavarr offered a hope-harvesting manifesto, wrapped up in delusional bravery. Bert Lavarr explained how to cheat death and still look normal while doing it. And the overall timing of the piece was perfect. Readers were tired of ingesting the same stories about mourners living lives of quiet desperation. Readers wanted an abnormal reaction, a refusal to accept the unacceptable, and an almost mentally unstable response to having one's world turned upside down when someone dies. They wanted to see the anomalous energy of heartbreaking denial continue to live forever. In short, they were tired of accepting the end of a story "as is." They wanted the left turn, so they had to know where the story came from in the first place. They begged their local bookstores to find this Bert Lavarr and promised to pay him anything if he would just come and save them from their hopeless, literary lives.

    The diner writer was initially embarrassed by the attention and was afraid to respond to it. He thought that if posted a graphic little story about a reporter who went undercover for six months in a mental instituition as a patient then he would get the readers to stop pouring out their hearts online. It did not have the effect he intended. The readers gobbled up this story as well and responded more fervently about this man then they did about the gentleman farmer. Finally, the very secret and private diner writer decided to accept a request from local publisher to put together a collection of these stories. The book received very positive reviews, but was still published under the pen name of Bert Lavarr. The success of the first collection allowed him to publish another few collections and then a short novel. The writer was now being paid to do what he would do for free. And it all started with the girl in the diner.

    So, when the frumpy little diner writer did happen to look up to take in his surroundings, the static in the room increased noticeably. It had always been nearly detectable to him before, but when he would see her, it spiked to uncomfortable levels. When he first caught her looking over at him, his eyes darted to the other four patrons what had shuffled in and slumped into the booths to see if they, too, felt the rogue wave of dangerous energy that had just rolled through the place. No one seemed to notice anything. The tinkling bell above the door that had alerted Vivian to a new arrival didn't seem an ominous precursor to anyone else that something cosmic was about to happen. He stabbed his right hand toward his nearest stub of his #2 pencil. With quivering fingers he forced himself to make a note why other people could not detect the unraveling of the universe.

    She was a shade over five feet tall. Perhaps she was a dancer. The legs that came out of her light purple petal summer skirt were smooth, toned, yet not overly muscular. He tried to revert his attention back to his journal, but despite the mental effort to complete his thought by writing it down, he kept looking up to see if she was still there. She was. She was bent over, peering into the glass case by the cash register that held the freshly baked muffins and scones. It was all for show, because she ordered the same thing every time.

    It was like his head was having a muscle spasm as it twitched up to see her and then back down to his writing. Down and up. As Vivian was ringing up other customers, a small line of patrons formed behind the young woman. They appeared to be perturbed that she couldn't make up her mind. An old woman in line scowled with impatience as she looked at her wristwatch and then out of the front window of the diner to see if her bus was approaching. An unshaven man in dirty clothes and heavy workbooks stood directly behind her and studied with lust the shape of the young woman's legs.

    What the angel at the display case, the four other diner patrons, Vivan herself, and the rest of the world didn't realize was that Bert Lavarr was no longer a mild-mannered accountant who had memorized whole sections of Oregon tax code and could script out spreadsheets like a baker sprinkles flour. He was a writer. He was Bert Lavarr; a refiner of identities and a biographer of human emotion. He was now a man doing what he loved to do.

    The young woman finally purchased her blueberry muffin and her extra hot mocha. As she walked toward the door, she paused at the disheveled space of artistic chaos that was Bert Lavarr. She smiled warmly at him. She disregarded the fears the other patrons had who gave the strange little man a wide berth like one would cross a street to avoid a homeless man wearing nothing but a ragged American flag. She sat at the adjoining table with her muffin in one hand and mocha in the other. She never sat down in the diner before.

"Good morning," she nearly whispered. "I always see you in here." She took a sip of her mocha as she looked into the man's confused eyes. "You look like a writer. I love to write, too. What are you working on?"

Channeling My Inner Bob

My brother and I were close once, about a hundred and fifty years ago, it seems. He is five years older than I am and usually included me in things he was doing with his friends, provided they didn't involve him having to act cool. It didn't matter to me though. I thought he was the boss; tougher than a box of sixteen-penny nails, with a raw, rusted edge to him. He'd never backed down to anyone or anything, which is somewhat admirable when you're twelve, but it would not serve him well later in life when it came to the high school administration staff, the local law enforcement, and our father.

But more than the scrappiness of the guy, I remember his dramatic and sensitive side. I remember once when we were playing together—he was about twelve and I was seven—we pretended we were young actors improvising stories like the ones we saw on TV or read about in books. We often ended up in momentous battles against overmatched forces. And when one of us would take the fatal, final blow (we normally took turns at who got the death-scene speech), the normal wartime brotherhood cheese-fest would commence:

Younger Brother: "You . . . <cough> . . . you'll always be . . . <cough> . . . my brother."

Older brother grasps the hand of the dying younger brother.

Older Brother: "Don't talk like that. You're gonna make it."

Younger Brother: "I . . . wish we coulda . . . went to . . . <final gasp of air> . . . Hawaiiiiiii . . . " *(Eyes remain open as life drains from face.)*

Older Brother: "Damn . . . " *(whispers)*

Fade to black. Cut! Print it! Tell the Academy we'll be in the bar when the Oscars arrive.

PeeeYuuuu. Who farted, right? The overacting was not wasted on us, that's for sure. But some forty years later, I still remember those makeshift moments spent with him. He was my first hero.

I wasn't born into the family that currently calls me their son and brother. My biological mother had an affair while she was married to her third or fourth husband, depending on which story she chose to tell you and which one you ended up believing. Regardless, she left their home as a result of her douchebag husband's verbal and emotional abuse. She packed up her five-year-old daughter from a previous marriage (my half-sister) and went to San Diego to spend time with a girlfriend. While she and her girlfriend were out one night, she met a dashing young Italian man singing and playing the guitar at a local nightclub. She ended up falling head over heels for the guy. They would spend the next few months together which culminated in her getting pregnant, the DEA arresting him for drug trafficking, and him being sent to prison. It's a fond little story that has a romantic yet "Tony Soprano" twist to it. As a result of his incarceration in San Quentin, she was forced to move back in with the aforementioned douchebag of a husband. The reunion was based on one life-changing condition: he would take her and her daughter back, but the bastard baby had to be either aborted or put up for adoption. Thankfully for my sake and my existence, she chose the latter.

In California at that time, adoptions were sealed. They might still be for all I know, but back then you couldn't find out who adopted your child and the adopted kid couldn't find out the identity of his or her birth parents. So the moment I came out of the womb, they hosed me off, slapped a little cotton blanket around me and whisked me off to the nursery. So quick was this transition from the womb to weight scale and then out the door that the bio-mom didn't even get to look at me or hold me. I know all of this information because the woman who adopted me was a nurse in the hospital in which I was born. Talk about getting front row seats to the show, right?

The young nurse put in for the adoption paperwork even before I was born, scooped me up upon approval, and took me home to her husband and their five-year-old son (the aforementioned piece of scrap iron/over-actor). I was raised in relative comfort and given all that I needed to survive: food, shelter, baseball gloves, record player, a Stretch Armstrong that I dissected on my tenth birthday, a homemade denim suit that I wore to my baptism, a whole stack of Elvis Presley albums, and a Farrah Fawcett poster. It wasn't such a bad way to grow up. If it wasn't sneaking the shots of Wild Turkey when I was ten years old, or the whacks with the jumper cables for losing a pair of pliers, I might have grown up to be President of the United States or something. It's the "or something" part that makes this a particularly funny story.

Anyway, my brother is Robert Rawlings, Jr., as in, the namesake of my father, Rober Rawlings, Sr. I used to look on that title as something that would be pretty cool to have. I thought perhaps the royals of England should have something like that but then decided against it. The cool factor goes out the window when you're "Prince Charles, Jr." In fact, when I was little, I wished that my father had called me something that would allow me to have a cool Roman numeral after my name, like Edward the Sixth, or Henry the Eighth, or Thurston Howell the Third. I used to think that being a "Jr." or a "Third" or something like that was the universal sign of being the exact same as the person before you. If my dad was "Sr." and my brother was "Jr." then in order for me to be like my hero (my brother), then I should naturally be "Norman Gilbert Rawlings, the Third". I wasn't that bright, apparently, because I didn't pick up on the fact that my brother and father shared the same name.

When someone finally told me how the naming convention worked, I remember being disappointed. That meant I couldn't be a "the Third" or a "Junior" or even the Prince of Wales. The latter realization particularly sucked because I was in love with Princess Diana of Wales at the time and I figured if she was going to marry a big-eared goober it might as well be me. But what it also did was put into my head the notion that, since my father didn't name me after himself, he must not have liked me very much. That false realization stung a bit. What kid doesn't like to think that he and his dad are pals, compadres, or buddies? I carried that ridiculous notion around for a few years until I found that my dad named me after a close, dear friend whom he respected and admired. But when you're six years old and think that Spiderman is real and Evel Knievel is Jesus Christ there's no telling what nonsense will take seed in the shallow topsoil of your mind. So, I grew up a Norman.

I didn't see the value in "Norman." I saw the nerd-like characterizations on television and heard the giggles in the classroom when I was forced to stand up and introduce myself at the beginning of each school year. And back in the day, the first few minutes of class on the first day of school were always reserved for roll call, and the class attendance sheet always had limited space in each box. This proved socially disastrous for me as my name inevitably got cut off at the very end. Thus, "Rawlings, Norman G." became "Rawlings, Norma". And if I didn't correct the teacher quickly, he or she would repeat in a louder voice, "Norma? Is there a Norma present?"

  A confidence problem began to fester. All from a simple and—as it turns out—honorable name. So, in order to overcome the problem, I begged my brother to create stories with me and act them out. It was the first step toward a creative existence that put me somewhere. . . anywhere. . . other than where I was actually living, and transformed me into someone. . . anyone. . . other than who I actually was.

  I'm not saying that my name was the root cause for the identify crisis I struggled with over the years, but I do know it played a pretty decent supporting role in it. I have, for the better part of my life, resisted who I am and what I needed to do to be happy. This confusion wouldn't serve me well as a son, brother, and friend, and it would eventually torture me as a husband and a father. It wasn't until my children were born that I started to see a path toward my missing identity, and when Teresa and I came back into each other's lives I discovered that the warm, calming waters of her presence were a much better place to become a man than the wide open, unknown highways and backcountry roads of my past.

  "Norman" and I have grown to appreciate one another. We have begun to recognize those subtle, arduous responsibilities that come with carrying a name like that around for fifty years. I've gotten a little better at it because I know that the name—in and of itself—does not define who I am, any more than "Maxwell" defines my son or "Morgan" defines my daughter. They are amazing humans: full of hope, passion, curiosity, a deep thoughtful intellect, and truck-loads of humor. But, as their father, I can't see them being named anything else. I suppose that would hold true for my parents when they think of me.

  Over time, I realized that the label of son and father, husband and brother, was more important than any name incorrectly announced by my elementary school teachers. For the record, I think those teachers knew exactly what my name was but were getting their digs in early because they knew what kind of kid they were taking into their class.

What "Norman" did teach me, however, was to look left to my past and right to my future to understand where my identity may reside, that is to say, where my center point or my fulcrum should be placed. And once that point is defined, the name that I was given doesn't seem to matter as much as I thought it did. I am starting to appreciate more the names to which I healthfully and joyously respond rather than the one on my birth certificate.

So, you can call me "Norman" or even "Norm" if you get the sense that I like you. After that, I'm open to whatever. Just don't call me late for dinner.

Words

Growing up, I had only one distinct rule instilled by my father when it came to communication: be brief and be truthful. I was raised by a former Marine who thought the only method of communication was epitomized by the heroes of the old Westerns on TV or the big screen: John Wayne, Clint Eastwood, and the Cartwrights. Yet ironically, there didn't exist any theatrical drama where I lived. There was no nuance in my house, growing up. You said what you had to say or you shut the hell up. Anything in between and you ran the risk of getting smacked upside the head.

As a young boy, there was always something charming to me when people turned a phrase or threaded some meaning a little deeper between the lines. I certainly wasn't one of those people initially. I didn't like being too wordy, actually. The neighborhood I grew up in didn't reward wit as much as it did raw brutality. And it wasn't because I didn't appreciate the layers that often go with communication. I think it was because I didn't understand that there were layers in the first place. I had to reread things over and over because I didn't pick up their backstage meaning or I tripped over the significance of the message the first time because I couldn't see it coming from six pages away.

But eventually I became drawn to words like a sleeping man is awakened by the smell of bacon frying in a pan. In high school I read more mature pieces even when I didn't understand what the hell they meant, stuff written by guys like Mickey Spillane and John Creasey, William Faulkner, Shakespeare, CS Lewis, and Sir Arthur Conan Doyle. Then, at the dangerous age of eighteen, I started reading Hemingway. To an eighteen-year-old punk with an axe to grind and who already possessed a wandering spirit, reading Hemingway might have been the worst idea imaginable. But in a way Hemingway grounded me and reminded me of home because he—like my father—had no interest in nuance, and after reading a lot of wordy, inflated stories from English authors, it was refreshing to swing to the Hemingway end of the spectrum. "Papa" made me feel like I hadn't wandered too far off the ranch.

Hemingway mentioned H.L. Mencken in one of his books, so I started reading Mencken. Oddly enough, Mencken's satire led to the hallof-fame stand-up comedian, George Carlin. It wasn't that difficult a leap to like Carlin's language, actually. Anyone who can use "fart, turd, and twat" in the same sentence would attract any goofy teenager. So both Mencken and Carlin taught me about the satirical rips of seasoned street poets: sharp, bitter, and cutting, to-the-point with just the right amount of raunchy language at just the right place to make you laugh when you shouldn't. George Carlin dropped all pretenses for me, and once his *Occupation: Foole* comedy album found its way to the turntable in my bedroom I knew I was hooked on words or, at the very least, the seven dirty ones you couldn't (and still can't) say on television.

Carlin's academic edginess and language turned me on to Douglas Adams and his *Hitchhiker's Guide to the Galaxy*. Adams told me to save time and "just go mad now," so I did, but in a less psychedelic sort of way. My "going mad" involved going quiet and swallowing all of the things that were going wrong around me and longing for the things that never seemed to go right, in order to be noticed by the people I wanted to impress. I don't believe it to be an accident, then, that Adams led to Kurt Vonnegut who, although also a satirist, liked to keep things simple. "The good Earth—we could have saved it, but we were too damn cheap and lazy." Even in my teenage and early adult life, all of this back-and-forth, serious literary exploration was sprinkled nicely with Maurice Sendak (*Where the Wild Things Are*), Robert W. Service (aka "The Bard of the Yukon"), A.A. Milne (*Winnie the Pooh*), and Shel Silverstein (*Where the Sidewalk Ends*). Besides, a guy can only take so much heavy shit before he needs a little "Let the wild rumpus start!" and "Once there was a tree. . . and she loved a little boy."

Once the books were in the bag, I started paying more attention to the tools of metaphors and similes, little utensils that hint but don't quite shove things down your throat. After a while, I wanted to learn about plot and dialogue, creating arcs and crests, evoking emotion and enriching characters. I wanted to learn how to infuse imagery and personify shadows. I also wanted to hear and smell the scenes before writing about any of them, so I drove to the mountains, the beaches, and a few times to the desert—alone—and let the landscape speak to me. I wanted all this stuff because anything, everything, had to be better than what was happening to me at the time.

After a while, I liked listening to people talk, and started to shut up more (my father would have been so proud). I discovered a whole population of people who had spent their lives becoming real characters with real personalities. They did so organically and not by studying language and reading books and rewinding scenes in movies like I had been trying to do. I was listening to verbal dialogue and siphoning diction out of the normal men and women I found on the streets of my hometown, but they were just talking and interacting and living their lives as normally as they knew how.

I went to the other side of the world to listen to people. I found some true characters there: stage directors, writers, readers, soldiers, actors, playwrights, musicians, painters, dancers, sculptors, and one very old, very fat, and very drunk Italian Santa Claus. I wanted to listen to them all because I thought that if I knew how to write and speak like they did then I would be able to tell people how I feel and then they'd like me, or at the very least, not want to hurt me.

In short, I guess I wanted to be smarter. I wanted to be able to describe what I was feeling. I wanted to recognize the voices that were pinging around in my own body, from the echo chamber of my skull, down the gravelly throat toward my impetuous heart, weaving through a scarred rib cage, dripping down into young legs and into second-hand ankles, and finally filling up larger-than-average big toes.

Ultimately though, I wanted to be someone else. And I didn't want to say things outright. I wanted to say them with style. I wanted to tell others about things without having to spell anything out for them. I wanted to slip a note across the years and tell some people how I really felt without coming right out and saying it because that would have gotten me laughed at, slapped, or both. I wanted to make people laugh at what I created and enjoy their moment of happiness while deflecting the lack of my own. I wanted to have someone (or even something) listen to me and reflect on what I said after I said it. And I wanted to cry without actually doing it.

And so I read. And I wrote. And after a few decades, I poured my guts out on some cheap notebook paper and off-white typing sheets. Without really intending to, or even having any sort of real plan, I put together a few stories that turned into a few books. I made them available to whoever wanted them. I continued to write stories, essays, poetry, and even some very nauseating haiku. For nearly all my life—through words—I've tried to get myself out there so others would appreciate me more without really identifying who I am in the process. It was the only way I knew how to dip my toes in the water of life while remaining cloaked under a shroud of secrecy and shame.

A comedy writer once interviewed a famous stand-up comic and asked him what his biggest fear was while on the stage. The comic said, "You would think it be bombing up there, or forgetting my bits, or the crowd not laughing at the right time or something like that. But for me . . . the thing that terrifies me the most is for the audience to become fully aware of who I really am." Like this comic, I would hide behind the words, for as brave as I thought I was, there is nothing like the blank page to pull over the top of your head and cower underneath. For the majority of my life, I've done a pretty decent job using my writing to put out a "voice" of who I am in order to define an image of what I wanted people to see. And just when I thought I finally had the right words in order and knew what to say and when to say it. . . I met Teresa again.

When she and I reconnected in my late forties (we had known one another peripherally in high school), I became fixated on getting her to understand who I was without going through all the old tricks I had once employed. I tried to write her notes and long sections of journal entries and poems. I even attempted singing a song to myself that encapsulated how I felt. The writings didn't do her justice, the poems were pure cheese, and the song should never be heard in public. . . by anyone. . . ever.

When my old fail-safe words didn't do the trick, I scrambled to be with her, just to hold her hand whenever I could, and to pull her to me. It's ironic, really. I spent most of my life reading, writing, and turning phrases into feelings to make things more understandable to myself, but ever since she started talking to me I've been hanging on *her* words. I praise *her* writing and *her* thoughts because even though she doesn't think so, I believe they are as poignant, dear, and heartfelt as anything I have ever read in my life. The words she tells me have reshaped the words I'm telling myself.

I like to walk with her. I like to ride in a car with her. I like to cook simple meals with her. I would drive five hours to hear her laugh, to see her sit at her kitchen table and cut out paper snowflakes for her students, or watch her sing as she runs on the treadmill for 30 minutes. I have never yet—and suspect I never will—got enough of being in her presence. And I will never be able to completely and thoroughly convey the love that she has reciprocated to me.

That's the benefit and byproduct of letters and words, sometimes. You can give something tangible to moments that are intangible. You can give physicality to fragments of time when everything else seems so ethereal. With words, you can sporadically toss in a little punctuation now and then, and sooner or later, inch your way closer to expressing something that has taken you a lifetime to suppress. And with all due respect to Gary Chapman and his book *The 5 Languages of Love*, I don't believe that words are ingredients of love. While I think that "Words of Affirmation" are important to communication (which is certainly important in developing a loving relationship), I'm a firm believer in the physical act of showing how far you are willing to go to love someone.

Love is action and words are intent. One is live giving and the other is wallpaper. But I suppose if you start to understand the words and use them in the right context and witness the effect they have on people, then perhaps love—or something like it—becomes a little more tangible. The words can become the marrow that creates the skeleton of our relationships, whether they be emotional, physical, or familial. Words are what we start with. If, for no other reason, simply to let us know we are not alone.

And if you can understand and appreciate the words of Dr. Scuss: "Today you are You, that is truer than true. There is no one alive who is Youer than You," then you are off to a pretty decent start.

The Big Reveal on Washington Street

"Wait. . . what? Are you serious?"

Shelly Jordan asked it with such incredulity that it nearly came out as a whisper. It almost made him believe that she had no idea what he was talking about. *Almost*, mind you. Not quite. . . but almost.

Adam shrugged nonchalantly. "Yeah, well. . . that's what the guy said to me and now I'm bringing it to you and I'd like to know what you're going to say to me. You know. . . 'benefit of the doubt' type of thing."

She sat glaring at him from across her three-onion vodka gimlet. At first, he looked at her squinting eyes and feigned incredulity with complete indifference. Then he glanced down at her drink like he had just noticed a ladybug on the table. What twenty-two-year-old from Dufur, Oregon drinks vodka gimlets, for God's sake? All in all, it was painful watching Shelly climb out of her contrived shock and come back to the reality of the question at hand. Not so painful, however, that Adam couldn't lift his beer to his lips and sip on it slowly while his questioning eyes never left her stare.

"You've got to be kidding me." Her eyes narrowed, darted to the left and right of his shoulders, and then back to his face. Adam instantly thought about that TV show that he'd been meaning to watch about people who can detect liars just by the way they adjusted their facial expressions, how their voice inflections changed, and how they manipulated items within their grasp. All telltale signs of a nervous individual searching for their own version of the truth. This, of course, would be useful information to draw from if he didn't already have pictures and a pretty clear video file of the event in question on his laptop. Nevertheless, he made a mental note to DVR the program about liars later that evening.

"Nope. Not kidding. Take another sip of your drink. You want to order something? Appetizers? Pork sliders? Perhaps a crème brûlée? Bottle of Krug? None of which I'm paying for, of course." He felt rather cool at that particular moment. He wasn't sure why, because the thought of losing her nagged at him. Nevertheless, he had bought into burning this bridge after long deliberations with himself. It made him wonder whether he was ready for any meaningful relationship, much less whatever the hell this one was supposed to be. But, much like the kid on the tire swing soaring out over the river, there was now only one way off the rope.

"I don't have to sit here and listen to this. I knew this was too good to be true. I'm seeing the darker side to you that *literally* everyone warned me about."

He nodded politely as he leaned slowly over the table towards her. "I think you are *literally* using the word 'literally' word incorrectly," he whispered. He straightened up and took another sip of his beer.

She started to get up when he slid a DVD across the table with all the juicy info that some guy named Mike had dug up for him at the Cinco de Mayo party she'd been at last week. Mike was a rather shadowy sort of character and were it not for his immaculate timing with his camera phone and a bitterness from being dumped by this same woman two years ago, Adam never would have given him the time of day. Not for any other reason than he just didn't trust the guy. Now Mike was his newest and bestest buddy and big toe.

"Oh, don't leave. Oh please, don't go. Oh golly, you're leaving? Oh gee, oh no. . . oh. . . hmmm." His artificial objection to her leaving had all the sincerity of an ATM telling him that he had insufficient funds in his account. Why did he like this side of himself so much? Ultimately, he figured that since this was not going to end well, then everything leading up to the end was all about the attitude. He might as well play the role. "Besides." He tapped the disc a couple of times with his fingers, "You'll want to take this with you. Ripping good stuff. It's amazing how clear you can get pictures and videos off cellphones these days, isn't it?"

As she glanced down at the disc, it occurred to her that her ploy of stomping out of the bar wasn't going to stick. She had been caught dead to rights in her own lie and despite the fact that the jury was ready to come back with a clear verdict, she wasn't going to go down without a fight. She took the disc, looked at it as if she were holding the tail of a dead rat she had just found under her sink, and with a dismissive little snort, flung it across a couple of tables, where it grazed someone's head before it smashed against the wall.

"Wow. Guess you didn't like that copy. No worries. I have about a dozen more. And you know another funny thing? I also have in my cell phone the email addresses and phone numbers of all our 'mutual' friends at church. You remember that church, don't you? The one where you volunteer in the children's ministry and the one you insisted I go to and the one you dragged me to for nine months of Sundays because you thought it would be 'good for my soul' and 'good for us' and all that happy horse shit?

"Anyway, I have a whole list of those hypocritical fuckers' cell numbers in my phone now and I'm sure they would love to see you perform the 'find the jello shooter' trick you were demonstrating on that guy at the Connelly party last Friday night. Which Friday night, you ask? The one where you said you were going to your mom and dad's place in Seattle because you missed them, and even cried a bit. That crying part was *brilliant*, by the way. You got me to hold you while you blew your nose all over my cashmere sweater. Epic, babe. Pure genius. Now. . ." He took another sip of beer and then wiped the corners of his mouth delicately with the cloth napkin he kept folded neatly on his lap, ". . . given that you didn't look too hammered in the video—pretty poised actually—and also that you got me to feel sorry for you about missing your folks, I'm not inclined to give you a free pass on your. . . how should I put it. . 'Easy' behavior? Speaking of videos, do you think YouTube likes stuff like this? I bet they would. I should probably figure out how to post this stuff, cuz I bet I'd get like a gajillion hits or something. I could be famous. Well. . . not as famous as you're going to be, of course but. . . " He took another long, thoughtful sip of his beer as he pretended to ponder the complicating process of posting videos to the internet.

When she didn't make a move toward the door, he set the beer down as his smiled hardened into a more menacing scowl. He stared into her defeated expression. "Look me in the eye and call me a liar."

She sat, and inhaled sharply. Her chin dipped to her chest as her eyes started to water. She was quite the princess. She bit her lower lip as her trembling hands dug through her purse to find her keys. After a few long, silent moments of his staring at her, she finally lifted her head and looked at him with an air of surrender. His intense stare, once fueled by poison, slowly melted away. He blinked and looked over the top of her head to the clock on the wall. He had been planning on this meeting for days. He spent hours on what he would say to her and all the possible responses she would give in trying to defend herself. Adam talked himself into and out of confronting her with this breach of trust and fidelity in their relationship several times. He wanted to give her all the time in the world to come to him and talk about the event and explain why she thought the relationship wasn't working and that "she needed space to find out who she was" or "it's not you, Adam…it's me." His gaze was fixed on the clock on the wall as he wondered how long it would take for the churning in his stomach to end and for the lump in his throat to dissolve. As he saw the second hand tick away, he noticed the movement of the patrons in the bar. His mind came back to the moment.

    He nodded to himself as his gaze fell back to her, this time with his own look of acceptance. The corners of her eyes finally let the few teardrops that were being imprisoned there slowly roll down her cheek. She stood up as proudly as she could, straightened her dress, and headed for the door. There was almost a misstep in her shuffle. He watched her walk out of the bar and across the street.

    Adam sat alone at the table. He understood that revealing this recent fracture in their relationship wasn't completely necessary. And it certainly wasn't necessary to reveal it in public and in such a theatrical manner. She probably would have ended up leaving anyway. They disagreed more than a couple in a new relationship should. He didn't believe in God and she spent the majority of her adult life pretending that she did. He could have just let her go. But he didn't like the idea of being beaten to the punch. That's how it had been lately. A fistfight where no one wins and both parties look like idiots as they drunkenly swing away at one another. She read a lot and tried to be a decent, upstanding, and a morally unreproachable woman. As it turned out, she kept books on finances that she never really comprehended, as well as soft porn novels that she, as it turns out, understood all too well. And as much as he had practiced the speech in his mind, the feeling that he thought he would experience after the great crescendo turned out to be less than satisfying.

She just made it so easy, at times, to want to go into battle. And that kind of zeal for conflict is not a healthy thing.

From his booth at the window, he saw her call for a taxi as she wiped more tears from her face. He suddenly felt all the eyes of the bar on him. They didn't seem to care as much about the past as he did. As he scanned all of the customers that were either embarrassingly looking over at the booth where the scene took place or staring at Adam to see what he was going to do next, he wondered if they could see the regret that was slowing creeping into his demeanor.

He finished his beer, dropped a twenty on the table, and walked toward the front doors. He stopped before the little steps that led to the exit and stared down at them. He looked at his watch and then looked back to the table where Shelly was last sitting. The rest of the patrons of the bar had now gone on with their conversations as if nothing had happened. The buzz of conversation blended in with the clattering of dishes and the piped in music playing somewhere in the bar. Without as much as a care or nod in the direction of his brokenness, the lives within the bar fell back into a chaotic rhythm.

Adam glanced back up at the clock on the wall of the bar. He turned slowly and made his way out into the dark street.

GREAT

You wouldn't really recognize him even after seeing him a dozen times. He blended into the scenery so well that it was only when he showed up on my doorstep the night of my brother's graduation party did I ever really see his face. On hindsight, I knew he was about the same age as me but at the time I didn't know what grade he was in or even if we went to the same school. He was nearly a ghost.

I opened the front door quickly as I was heading out to the car to get the last of the groceries my mom had bought for the party. I ran right into him. "Oh, wow! I'm sorry! Can I help you with something?"

He peered over my shoulder into the warm light of the living room like a hungry child would look at a tray of warm rolls through a bakery window. He looked back up at me and for the first time in my young life I was taken aback by the depth and intensity he had in his expression.

"Um, No. No, I was just…you guys having a party, huh?" He showed no remorse in being caught peeking through the small square window on our door. It seemed like he had something desperate he wanted to say but couldn't find the words.

"Yep, we are." I nodded over my shoulder toward the kitchen. "My older brother is graduating high school."

He closed his eyes and nodded knowingly. "Oh sure. Martin Allen Waite. Great ball player. Good arm. Turns a nifty double play."

I started to agree out of habit as I knew that everyone in town and all of my classmates knew who my older brother was but then stopped suddenly with a look of surprise. "How did you know Marty's middle name?"

The boy opened his eyes suddenly and snapped his gaze from past me to down to his feet. Without saying anything further he mumbled "Happy graduation to him" and quickly bolted from the porch and up the street away from the street light and into the darkness of the neighborhood.

It was three months before I saw him again. I was walking back from the corner store with two pockets of caramels and slurping on a bottle of Mountain Dew when I saw an ambulance and police cars with their lights on outside of a house a few blocks from where I lived. My curiosity carried me down amongst the onlookers and as I was surveying the scene I saw that same kid sitting in the middle of the side yard of the neighboring house with his back up against a tree. He saw me, stood up quickly, and ran through the narrow opening between both houses. I asked an older kid from the neighborhood what had happened.

"Don't know," he muttered "but they just pulled a dead body out of that house. Cops are asking a bunch of questions to everybody. Nobody knows nothin'."

"What about him?" I pointed in the direction of the disappearing figure scurrying away.

"That retard doesn't know shit. Can't tie his own shoes without falling over himself."

I turned away from the crowd and walked a few steps before looking down the narrow space that separated the two buildings. I saw him again. He was sitting cross legged with his back to the street and his head in his hands. Every fiber in my body told me to keep walking but for the life of me—up to this very day—I don't know what made me turn in his direction. I walked up slowly behind him and knelt down to his level.

"Hey. You ok?"

He gave a startled look and rubbed his bloodshot eyes; eyes that had looked like they hadn't felt sleep in days. They were puffy eyes but still focused and sharp. "Oh yes. I'm ok" he said. "What a silly question."

I smiled at his response. For some reason, hearing the word "silly" come from a ten year old was funny to me. "What happened here? Do you know?"

He looked down between his feet and fingered circles in the dirt with is finger. He shrugged. "Dad punched Mom again. Mom shot Dad. It's a pretty simple thing really."

I gasped quickly and looked through the side of the house, trying not to imagine the horrors that took place on the other side of the wall. After a few moments of breathless silence, I looked back at him. "I'm Eric."

He looked up at me. "I know."

"Yea, Ok. What's your name?"

He sighed deeply, almost disgustingly. He stood to his feet, faced me and held out his hand in the most formal manner I've ever seen a kid display. "I'm Gilbert Ramone Elizabeth Arthur Torrence." He shook my hand firmly as he looked me dead in the eye.

"Wow! That's a mouthful to…" I paused as I squinted back at him. Before I could put the thought together in my head, he beat me to the punch.

"It spells out G.R.E.A.T. But you can call me Gib."

For the next two years, Gib and I saw more and more of one another. He was the adopted son of a logger and a part time librarian. It turns out his mother had miscarried three times before finally deciding to adopt. The tolls of the deaths were, apparently, too hard on the father. He took to drinking heavily and was prone to violent spasms of rage. After years of beating his liver, his wife, and his son (in that order), that summer afternoon was the final climax of his self-destruction. The whole family had had enough. The coroner took away the father. The sheriff took away the mother. Eventually, she came back but to this day, I don't know if Gib lived alone in that house while she was gone or not. As for the murder, that's all that I remember and Gib never mentioned it again.

As it turned out, we did go to the same school. The school administrators had put Gib in the "special class" which meant to the rest of the kids that he was slow. Actually, he was the sharpest kid I had ever known. He knew facts about things that my parents didn't know. He played chess by himself in the cafeteria or at recess and was always reading something. Sooner or later, the geniuses in our school district realized he was smarter than they pegged him for. By the time he was in high school he was sitting next to me in almost every class and breezing through subjects that were putting me to sleep. We rode to high school together every day; first on the bus and then when I got my driver's license I'd swing by that same house where his mother shot his father. He was always sitting on the front step. His mother would sit next to him with a mug of coffee rolling between her two hands. Whenever I pulled up, he would stand, kiss his mother on the forehead, and then walk quickly to the car. He was the only kid I ever knew that kissed his mom in public.

I found his company to be calming. He never really got upset about anything. His favorite response to my ravings about homework, girls that wouldn't notice me, or the crappy hot lunches was the same each and every time: "Let it play out, kid. Why worry about it?"

Graduation came and went for both of us. Despite a near perfect SAT score and dozens of academic offers from colleges, Gib decided to stay in our hometown and work at the local mill. He became a repairman of the giant machines that kept the mill running and half the town employed. I went off to the state college to pursue a degree in teaching. I met my wife there; we got married and had a son named Gus. A few years after college, we moved to the next state over to go to graduate school together. Years had passed before I heard from Gib again. Correspondence between the two of us slipped away. Memories that involved our time together – as they often do – started to collet cobwebs and dust like unread books on a shelf.

My wife and I came home for Christmas one year. My mom met us at the door with a big hug. She immediately took Gus from my arms, squeezed him and then started making those ridiculous farting noises into the nape of his neck; sounds that only grandmothers can make. As my wife and I were hugging all the family members that had congregated at the house for the holiday, my mom stood among all of them, pulled me a little closer to her by putting her hands on my shoulders, and solemnly said "Eric? Honey…Gib was shot and killed last week."

The rest of the house guests and family members all fell immediately silent. Even the Christmas music that mom had perpetually playing in the kitchen seemed to fade away with the dull ringing in my ears. I dropped the diaper bag I was holding and slumped to the couch. Her words hovered in the room like cigar smoke; not rising or falling but just drifting ominously above our heads. He was shot by a local meth addict for $40 cash and a backpack full of books as he was walking through the local park on his way home from the night shift at the mill.

I excused myself from the group and went out onto my mother's back deck and wept. For the first time in my life, I cried openly from a sense of loss that I couldn't explain. I really don't know why it struck me so hard. Gib and I hadn't spoken in years. I received several letters from him after high school. I responded to most all of them but after a while my workload and my personal life took over my schedule to the point where writing an old friend became less and less a priority. I even received a letter from him a few weeks before Christmas. I threw it in my briefcase, intending to read it when I had more time. It was still in my briefcase which was in the car. I went to the car and opened it. After a few basic details, I came across a sentiment that summed up how Gib's mind seemed to work:

Eric? Have you ever noticed that people seem to lose interest when it comes from thinking to talking to doing? Why do you think that is? It's like they have a hook in the water, a fish is on it, and as they are reeling it up into the boat they drop the pole into the water and start yodeling. It's not like the thought has to race around the universe before it gets to your mouth. It is lightning fast going from your brain to your hands. And yet people just forget what they are doing or neglect to follow through on things.

Just yesterday, I was talking to ol' Bill McClaine. You remember, Billy? He left town for a while and then came back with half of his hair and twice the belly he had in school. Anyway, Bill was supposed to run over to Tacoma to get some lubricants for the saws in tower two and he just plain forgot. He had one job to do. He just forgot. So Mr. Peterson fired him. I saw him at the supermarket a few days later and you know what he said to me? "I got sidetracked." What does that even mean? That's silly to me. Just plain silly...

When are you coming back to town?

The next morning, Gus was up before anyone else in the house. I kissed my wife as she lay sleeping, picked him up out of his travel crib, and dressed him in his warmest clothes. We quietly tiptoed out into a crisp, cold morning. The sun was barely rising as I loaded Gus into his car seat. We went to the cemetery together where Gib's mother had buried him. There were fresh flowers on his grave. They had a frost on them but their color remained vibrant. As I held my young son, I looked down at the tombstone expecting to be filled with more confusion and anger. For the first time since I was a young boy, I prayed to God. I prayed for some answers to my questions. I prayed for a happier thought to reach my mind than the images I was having of my childhood friend lying rotting beneath the earth. I prayed that my son would never feel this kind of ache in his life.

I did not receive any comfort. I felt no wave of peace roll over me. The clouds didn't open up and no music played softly in the background of my mind like it does in the movies. I felt no resolution or finality, but what I did feel was nausea. I closed my eyes to remember the moment I first met Gib. I thought of the complexity of his childhood; how he came out of such a graphic tragedy and yet still had such a caring heart and a deep well of intelligence and forgiveness. I was even sickened by the fact I had to use the past tense when thinking about my friend. I was ashamed that I did not fully commit to our friendship over the last few years.

I opened my eyes and saw Gus staring at me. As he sucked on his pacifier, he carefully surveyed my face and rubbed his tiny fingers over the stubble of my whiskers. I kissed the palm of his hand as I looked down to Gib's headstone. On it was his long list of names etched in white amongst the black marble. I recalled the first time he introduced himself to me and how formal it was and how brave it must have been to meet someone new only hours after his mother killed his father. There was no date of his birth or death on the headstone. There was no reference to him being "A Loving Son" or "Friend to All." But as I was about to turn away my eyes caught a smaller inscription below Gib's long list of names. A sliver of light broke through the wretched maelstrom howling through my mind. A smile slowly formed at the corners of my mouth. I snorted at what I read as my emotions rose up into my throat.

Etched in smaller white lettering upon black marble, were three simple words; from the mind to the mouth and from the mouth to some carver's hands.

He was GREAT

"Yea…" I nodded slowly, squeezed my son in my arms, and walked back to the car.

Pagliacci the Clown

On August 11, 2014, the actor and comedian, Robin Williams, was found dead in his home in Marin County, CA. At the time, this news really bothered me, although I'm not sure why. I was a fan of his since his television days of playing the beloved alien Mork along with his sidekick Mindy. I loved his comedy album *Reality: What a Concept*, and a few one-liners from his occasional HBO standup specials found their way into my common vernacular.

But in all honesty, I didn't expect him to live as long as he did. I always thought he was almost too meteoric to last. No one seemed capable of sustaining that kind of explosive energy. Williams was pals with Andy Kaufman. He worked at The Comedy Store in Los Angeles with Richard Pryor. He was around the most brilliant comedic minds of his generation, and not only held his own but often blinded them with his own brilliance. He also was sucked up into the horrid addictions that claimed some of those lives. He was with John Belushi the night Belushi overdosed. Somehow, he found a way to rise above all of that and battle on. So, in a simple sense, I felt a familiar connection to the man.

The more I heard of the crushing yoke of depression and constant battle with addiction that Williams struggled with for the majority of his adult life, the more I was reminded of the old story about the guy who goes into a doctor's office:

A man is completely distraught. He can barely stop crying as he explains to the doctor that he is horribly depressed. He tells his doctor that his life is cruel and harsh and that he feels so utterly alone, even among a room full of admirers.

The doctor listens attentively and responds, "The treatment is simple. The great clown, Pagliacci, is in town tonight. Go to one of his shows. He will certainly lift your spirits."

The man erupts in another deep fit of sobbing. The doctor says, "What is wrong now?"

*The man says, "Doctor . . . **I am** Pagliacci."*

It doesn't take a concerted effort to discover that souls sometimes get lost when they engage in dangerous distractions. It affects not just the rich and famous. It's our neighbors, our classmates, our coworkers, and our family. Depression kills all of us a little bit at a time. And when it is discovered to have been the culprit for such a beloved entertainer, it bridges the gap between Hollywood and Hometown, USA.

Robin Williams was an innovator and a comedic genius. I heard someone mention that the boundary most brilliant performers have in their minds—that borderline that tells others that they have gone too far artistically and should retract their energies —did not exist with Williams. To him, that borderline was nothing more than a yellow streak of urine upon new fallen snow. He constantly crossed that boundary to see how far he could push the envelope and how obscure he could get.

Late night talk show legend David Letterman worked with Robin Williams when they were both starving comedians performing for free drinks at The Comedy Store in Los Angeles in the 1970s. Letterman recalled the first night he saw Williams on stage. Williams was introduced as being from Scotland for some reason, so out of professional curiosity, Letterman and a few of his colleagues stuck around to watch the newcomer. They expected him to bomb in front of the notoriously tough crowds that The Comedy Store brought in on a nightly basis. As Letterman sat slack-jawed watching the cosmic force of Robin Williams onstage, he jokingly confessed to himself that there was no real point in continuing in show business. "If this guy is the bench mark, then I'm finished in this business" he recalled. Letterman went on to define himself and all of his fellow comedians as "the morning dew" whereas Williams was "a hurricane."

But despite all of this talent, Williams was a powerful mental force operating within a flawed physical shell. It seemed to me that the physical could not contain the spiritual. And I don't mean spiritual in the religious sense, but in an otherworldly one. The energy that kept trying to destroy Williams from the inside out—through addictions and over-indulgence—was arguably the same energy that kept us laughing hysterically and shaking our heads in disbelief. And if it *wasn't* the same energy, then they were bastard cousins, twice removed. All the while, the human vessel that held this otherworldly energy captive did so for sixty-three human years.

And if you put that kind of cosmic power in any kind of earthly container then it will, eventually, become corrosive and find its way out to the light of day. In short, Robin Williams was indeed cosmically gifted but painfully human.

A comment online regarding his death struck me rather brazenly one morning a few weeks after it happened. The world was still reeling from the news of his suicide and talk shows, internet sites, and tabloids were trying to make sense of it all. The comment I found, however, hit me right where I was living at the time and I haven't been able to get it out of my head since. The blogger posted that Williams was like a man riding an untrained horse riding on the edge. Whether it was the edge of life, happiness, or sanity was not clearly stated by the author. The piece went on to suggest that Williams would skim on the edge of control while we all would marvel at his courage, his daring and his brilliance. But at other times, the horse went where the horse wanted and Robin could only hang on for dear life. The author goes on to say that had Williams been able to control this ride, in essence, if he could have trained the horse, then it may have been a reminder to him that there is always something that can be done when faced with being out of control.

There is always something that can be done when faced with being out of control.

I used to take counseling sessions a decade ago or so. Actually, as a result of a few weekends that I don't seem to remember, the state of Washington was kind enough to invite me to these sessions. The state pointed out that I didn't suffer from an addiction as much as full-on abuse. I know this because the just-out-of-grad-school counselor suggested that it was abuse rather than addiction, and since the state of Washington puts a clear and legal delineation on the difference, they thought it best for me to go to counseling rather than jail. Counseling would teach me the differences between addiction and abuse. Jail would teach me to open up and say "aahh." I preferred the former, thank you very much.

It was sweet of the state of Washington to define these things for me really, but I didn't have the heart to tell them that it probably wasn't necessary to instruct me that drinking a bottle of cabernet sauvignon after priming the pump with a couple of double Crown Royals was hazardous to my physical and emotional well-being. But since I didn't do it every night, nor did I yearn to wake up in the morning and fill my coffee mug with tequila and orange juice that firmly put me in "abuse" category. Anyway, I went to these classes and they told me about some nifty little tricks of the trade to keep my mind occupied and away from the triggers that swamp alcoholics on an hourly basis. Little things such as:

1. When you see an advertisement for your favorite alcoholic beverage, think of a few positive yet completely abstract things that you could possibly be doing and then make a mental list of reasons *why* you're not doing them.

Excuse me? The great state of Washington wanted me to think of why I wasn't eating a tub full of black licorice or standing in line waiting to get into a Taylor Swift concert? Because thinking about those acts make me physically nauseous and are clearly the last things I'd be doing at any given point. I suppose Washington thought that if I was thinking of *why* I wasn't doing those things, then my mind wouldn't be focusing on the advertisement and therefore not thinking about drinking. It's flawed logic, of course, because I'd have to be freaking hammered to be spending money on Taylor Swift tickets in the first place.

Another little nugget of the state's wisdom was this one:

2. Call a friend and ask him or her out for a non-alcoholic beverage.

A rather innocuous suggestion, but again. . . flawed. My "friends" at the time were the boozy ones who were driving me to drink in the first place. So giving them a call and asking them out for coffee was akin to leaving the door open to the chicken coop and asking the coyotes to lock up when they were finished. I'm not blaming the coyotes. I blame the chickens.

Nevertheless, I was keen on trying to get a handle on my life so I attended the sessions with an open mind. Grad school counselor Bob wanted to find unique ways to assist me and the others who, either voluntarily or by mandate of the state, had to control the beasts that controlled them. He wanted to teach us to train that horse and give us some more positive options when life seemed to get out of control. Sometimes those unique ways helped me. Sometimes they didn't. I can't say whether or not they helped any of the others. At that moment, I was only concerned with what I needed to do to keep from drowning, but over time I thought how vital it was for some of the others in my little group to get a grasp on their demons, too. My demons were very annoying and caused undue strife and grief in my life. Some of theirs were flat-out murderous, and hell-bent on destroying them from within.

I believe there are moments in life where tools, exercises, and safety nets just don't work. I've always thought it insanely egotistical and grossly vain to try to change the fabric of human nature. We are God's design, after all. And if you believe that theory then it isn't such a far stretch to think that God makes perfect souls but imperfect embodiments in which they are carried.

I understand the flip sides of the argument: Does God make men and women dangerous drunks? Does God go about designing some to be addicted to meth or heroin? Are God's designs flawed and therefore is our perception of God flawed? I don't know those answers, but I doubt our ability to fully understand such lofty, cosmically unfathomable topics in the first place. Even an atheist would question a frog's ability to do long division.

What I do believe is that we are imperfect physical structures based on perfect architectural drawings. These thoughts help me find the answers when no one else can. Not Billy Graham or Bono, not the Bible or the obituaries. Nice plans. Crappy framework. Any good carpenter will tell you a house built like that won't stand for long. And so you don't have to believe in a higher power to understand that Robin Williams possessed a gift few people had. He entertained us. He made us laugh. He made us stare in disbelief and say, "My God, what the hell is he going to do now?"

He was given the gift and I don't think his shell knew how to handle it. It exploded out of him like fireworks in a blackened sky. You never knew what was going to happen next. He didn't either, as it turned out. You can't train that sort of horse. You can't fence in that kind of energy. It was one billion times more powerful than the house which held it. He fought to keep a safe containment on it for years.

I imagine he said, "I'll try *this*," because the last thing didn't work to quiet his thoughts. Williams once said that he didn't do cocaine to get crazy. He took cocaine so he could be quiet. He took it to "shut down the engine." If that internal thing can't be shut down despite the most powerful narcotics, what do you think is going to happen when the case carrying it finally starts to crumble?

Despite the brutal images of the last moments of his life and the internal battles he faced throughout a brilliant career, I'd like to think of Robin Williams's gift of comedy and artistic expression as an art, or even as something holy. Within his genius, perhaps subconsciously, Williams thought that the gift wasn't supposed to rot away in the shell. Perhaps he discovered that it was never going to fade away regardless of how drunk or high he got, or even how long he stayed sober. Maybe he recognized that the casing was falling apart. Maybe he knew that with the death of the shell, the spirit and the gift within would return to the place whence they'd come.

Maybe he thought that somewhere his gift could survive without a body.

Maybe he saw that somewhere in the realm of the unearthly, his gift would find another host to inhabit, and infect that being with unbridled joy.

Maybe that "somewhere" is a place where laughter echoes within the pillars of hope.

Maybe it is a place where positive, creative energy rips through the skies and lands beside embodiments of pure love and unyielding friendship.

Maybe it is a place where dreams come true.

Return if possible, Pagliacci.

The Window Pain

He must have passed that window a dozen times in the last few months. At first—being self-conscious about the man that he was—he walked by and, with his peripheral vision, sneaked a glimpse of his profile. He was a borderline narcissist, but mostly wanted to make sure his hair wasn't sticking out at obtuse angles or that he didn't have a dried booger hanging from his nose. Childhood fears lathered up with a healthy dose of vanity, but they originally evolved from taking too many smackings on too many playgrounds. No one liked the shy kid with the dried booger hanging from his nose.

But after a while, looking through his own reflection, he saw her. She was a petite figurine of a woman with such an outward warmth that a vapor trail of energy that to follow her when she walked. Her smile cut through the shadows of the poorly lit shop. After seeing her, he would slow his pace and blatantly look through the glass. Then, he pretended to take calls on his phone so that he could stop, turn toward the window, and look at her while pretending to look past her. But he wasn't looking past her. She raised her head and smiled at him, which made the blood rush to his face and flex his toes inside his bulky Doc Martins.

Doc Martins (and other heavier types of footwear) were another insecurity of childhood. They sprang from the moment his mother accidentally bought him womans' shoes at a flea market because they cost only two dollars (she haggled down from the listed five dollar price), and her son needed something other than his crusty canvas sneakers with holes and melted wax on the bottom. His mother was all about efficiency and thrift, but when the young boy stood on the playground during that first recess in those shoes, he immediately embraced the newly discovered term "self-defense." At that moment he made a pact with himself: no more gender-ambiguous footwear. Go big or go home.

On the 100th pass, he slowed before the door and decided to go in and pretend to browse about the shop. Since it was a woman's consignment store he knew that his ruse would be discovered immediately. So he took another phony phone call and stayed in front of the entrance for twenty minutes.

He looked at her. He looked away. He looked over the top of her but then settled his eyes on her angelic face. Her name tag said "Teresa."

"Of course," he sighed. He thought of no other name to befit such a classically gifted beauty. She was rain and the new sun afterwards. Then he thought that description too cheesy, and he started to think of her as the first few chords of his favorite song. Then he couldn't remember his favorite song because he was mesmerized by her eyes and the way her mouth moved when she talked to customers. He continued his charade, speaking words into the phone that had lost its battery power hours ago.

"My name is Norman," he said to no one but the dead phone. "I've been coming by your store for weeks now. I don't think you've noticed me. I understand if you haven't. I am a fool for standing out here. But I really have been coming here for weeks. I wish you'd notice me." He switched the phone to his other ear and gesticulated madly with his free hand as if making a comical point to the imaginary caller on the other end. "So here's the thing. I don't do well with first impressions and I would really like to make a good one with you. I want to come in and say hello and perhaps ask you if you would like to get a cup of tea or maybe a sandwich sometime. . . or something." He lowered his head as if the next few statements resonated with vital importance. "I was just thinking that maybe you saw me, too . . . you know, through the glass . . . and wondered if I was someone . . . you know . . . you would want to meet, or whatever."

He lifted the phone away from his face in disgust at his sheepishness. He grimaced and changed hands and turned away from the glass. "Or whatever? God, what am I, twelve years old? I guess I was just wondering if you could look at me for a few seconds so I could see how rich your eyes are. I like when your hair is up, but last Tuesday in the morning it was down, and you had on a cream-colored scarf. I don't know if anyone has ever told you this, but you can wear anything and you will look breathtaking and perfect and classical and lovely."

He turned his back to the glass, watched a bus drive by slowly, and followed it with his eyes, shrugging as if resigned to the next statement from the no one on the other end of the dead phone. "I'm not a stalker, although it probably looks like I am right now." He shook his head slightly and whispered into the dead mouthpiece, "And I don't know anything about love at first sight. I have never missed a woman before so I don't know. In fact, I don't think I've ever really missed anyone before . . . except for my kids, but they don't count 'cause I can miss them even when they're in the same room with me. And I generally don't keep people in my head. I keep thoughts in my head and recipes and maybe a poem or two and the quotes from books that I like. I think holding hands in public is a strange custom. I like big dogs and think people who keep birds are doing both themselves and the birds a huge disservice. I like pasta and ice cream and medium-rare steaks and if I thought I could get away with it and survive past fifty, I'd put butter on just about everything."

He turned back toward the shop where she was hanging lights around the front window. He caught his breath. It was the closest he'd been to her since he started walking past her shop. She looked at him and smiled and gave her hand a little flip of a wave. He waved back awkwardly and grinned without opening his mouth. He whispered into the dead phone to the no one who wasn't there.

"But I am in love with you, I'm pretty certain of that. I'm in love with you. . . the little, perfect woman in the little, perfect shop. So. . . you know . . . that's it, I guess." He closed his phone, looked ahead to where he thought he needed to go, and glanced back to where she had been standing only feet from him on the other side of a clean shop window. Inhaling deeply, exhaling likewise, he took a half step away from the door and then paused and bit his lower lip. He turned on his heels slowly, back toward the door, and closed his eyes and prayed a half-second prayer that seemed like the right thing to do but he never really could figure out why. Gripping the knob tightly, he pushed the door open.

The little bell rang to announce his presence. She turned around and smiled warmly.

Science, Seagrams, and George Carlin

I have been thinking lately, trying to remember if my father taught me anything that stuck. These thoughts haven't been all-consuming mind benders that have taken up great gobs of my day, nor have they really taken center stage in my thought process. It's been more like an Off-Broadway stage. Or maybe even the *way* Off-Broadway stage; the stage where you can see a one-legged Chinese rodeo clown singing show tunes while balancing on a pink exercise ball. For the record, I would *totally* pay the $3 cover charge to sit through that.

Anyway, the thought of attaching my dad to some tangible lessons has occupied my thoughts. And I have come to the pliable conclusion that the general indifference I had for his parenting ability made that scenario unlikely. It's not that I didn't love the guy. I really did . . . sort of . . . although I had trouble liking him most of the time. The reason that I have been thinking on whether my dad taught me anything tangible is that I don't think it actually happened. Perhaps I was too mentally and emotionally rebellious as a teenager to listen to anything the man had to say. Furthermore, I have always had a difficult time respecting someone who treats themselves with such reckless disregard. And I certainly had a hard time respecting someone who treated me with, at times, a baseless violence people usually reserved for dogs that shit on carpets and chew on new boots.

It's like the memory students have of their worst teacher ever, old Mrs. Whatsherface. You remember the one? She smelled like Pinesol and farted when she walked. "She was a bitter old clam and I didn't learn dick from her," you'd drunkenly reminisce at your ten-year reunion. But upon a more honest and retrospective examination, because of Mrs. Gimpy-Toots you know that there are fourteen punctuation marks in the English language. You know that "To be or not to be" is Shakespeare and "Always do sober what you said you'd do drunk" is Hemingway. Because of her, you understand that words have power and using them correctly, in the right order, and with a certain amount of poetic structure, can actually change someone's heart and mind. You know that stuff now, but back at your ten-year reunion you'd forgotten it because there was an open bar for the first half hour and all you remember is that her breath smelled like tuna fish and menthol and that she wore the same gaudy, turd-shaped pendant every day of your freshman year in high school.

Maybe that is how it was with my old man. On paper, the guy lived the typical American blue-collar life. In fact, on the surface, he was one of those exemplary types of fathers. He volunteered to umpire Little League baseball games, never missed showing up for my or my sister's sporting events, always put food on the table, and kept the house warm and dry. Many fathers I know have failed at these simple requirements because their selfish behavior got in the way and took them down dangerous little rabbit holes. As a result, their kids suffered. On paper, my old man wasn't that bad a guy; a very respectable father and a very respectable man.

But when the people in your life—the ones who mean the most to you and carry the most influence—are altered by booze, the memories of those moments are usually very good or very bad. There are silly happy memories of house parties, and drinking stories that make you shake your head and giggle. And there exist episodes that represent the polar opposite of those things. You don't reflect fondly on those silly moments. You may shake your head but in an incredulous, disbelieving sort of way. And you sure as hell don't giggle.

Upon stumbling across those memories as an adult, you are forced to travel way back to the abandoned acreage of your mind, past the house you grew up in, the garage that you always wanted to forget, and the yard that you slept in at times. You venture deep into the subconscious, uncharted, unexplored territory of your psyche, and once there, you dig a shallow grave and bury those memories. You bury that shit alive if you have to. You don't put up a marker because you hope to never find it again. But like Poe's tell-tale heart, the pulsating reminders of those events find you in your sleep or in your relationships with your wife or during the moments with your own children. The hurt and disgust bleed to the surface like rancid sweat from a long night of brown liquor shots and garlic sesame chicken, and then the memories start all over again.

That is what too much drinking does to some people. If used in sufficient quantity over long periods of time, alcohol can strip away our dignity and polish away the personality that makes some of us acceptable in public. Too much of it, for too long, exposes the bare skeleton of our animalistic nature. For some, it simply ruins the furnace of imagination. For others, alcohol fuels it but in ways that are unnatural and obscene. For my dad, I think that the thousands of beers, the decades of four-finger glasses of Seagram's whiskey and 7Up, and the weekday thermoses of coffee and Kahlua became a biological problem, a dangerous chemical reaction in what eventually would become an unstable laboratory. This scientific analogy reminds me of what the late, great comedian George Carlin used to say about his own father. It was a comical spin on a common disease. "My father," Carlin wrote, "had a challenging time metabolizing ethanol."

Carlin's light twist on dark matter illuminated a biological theory that seems to elude the subsection of society that classifies alcoholics as weak-minded losers with no self-control and a criminal lack of discipline. Frankly, I don't know why some people have the perception that alcohol addiction *isn't* a disease. After all, methanol, the simplest form of alcohol, is a chemical compound. What the funny beer commercials, the wine snobs, and James Bond and his "skaken, not stirred" martini guzzlers won't tell you, however, is that methanol is also used to make formaldehye and rocket fuel. And when it is bound to a second carbon atom it becomes the compound we know and love as ethanol. If you, like me, had trouble with basic chemistry in high school, try to remember what a college professor told me about the differences between the two. "Ethanol and alcohol are the same. It's just that ethanol wants to look more scientific so it wears a white lab coat and walks around with a clipboard." And if since all you have to do is add that one carbon atom to such a toxic liquid like methanol in order to make ethanol—and since humans are carbon-based life forms (any good alien in a sci-fi movie will tell you that)—it's not difficult to imagine the damaging long-term effects that take place when you mix the stuff together in a beaker and pour it into, over, and through live tissue for four to six hours a day, seven days a week, every day of the year. . . for fifty years.

After assigning some basic junior high school chemistry, the lesson gets easier to understand. Take a glass of alcohol, add oak-barrel seasoning, sprinkle in some cinnamon or whipped vanilla flavoring, add it to carbonated water with a twist of lime, and voila. . . you have a chemical compound that can make people drop their pants and poop off an overpass, or pick a fight with four extremely large Italians in Rome in front of a statue of Saint Jude (ironically, the patron saint of lost causes).

It's easier for me to come to this scientific conclusion rather than the alternative explanation. That is, that human beings are—at their most carnal, most basic form—no damn good. Some people shouldn't drink too much. That is obvious to anyone who giggles at wedding reception videos on YouTube. More sobering is that some of us can't drink at all without it changing our personalities into something unrecognizable to the people who love us the most.

I don't really know which category I am in. Not being biologically related to the man who adopted me and whom I called "Dad" my entire life, I don't have any genetic history to explain away the indecencies I've been a part of, contributed to, or manufactured on my own while—as the Bible says—"sitting too long at my wine." I suppose I hover somewhere in between "can't" and "shouldn't". And since it always has produced sandpaper-like results in my life—results that are gritty, uncomfortable, and unrecognizable—I have come to the conclusion that it's probably best I forego all the marketed benefits and stick to metabolizing a couple of hydrogen molecules with a schosh of oxygen just to round things out. Good ol' H20 wins out in the end.

Finally, in my father's defense (and Lord knows there were times he needed a good defense), he came to this very same conclusion later on in his life as well. Whether he had a change of heart or whether his body's failing health made up his mind for him is somewhat irrelevant. All I know is that a few years ago, the two of us locked ourselves in a back room (the same back room that you will read about later in this book) and, without really revealing the past and apologizing or explaining away the behavior, found our own versions of forgiveness and acceptance. That happens between fathers and sons sometimes.

The conversation didn't go how I thought it would. As someone who likes to imagine scenes and put words and dialogue to them, I would have scripted it out *considerably* differently than how it actually went down. But over time, the more I think about the conversation and the more I associated it with actual events in our shared past, the more I realize there was no other way the scenario could have happened than the way it did. Sometimes the actual truth is boring, but so absolutely necessary. We began to understand one another. And in doing so, we rediscovered that shallow grave on the back acreage of both of our subconscious minds and collectively put our tell-tale hearts to rest.

So, from that conversation with my old man (and from the years of drinking since I was 12), I learned that hereditary traits aren't always genetic. Sometimes, it all comes down to just plain chemistry regardless who your parents are. I learned that a simple conversation can go a lot farther and much deeper than one thinks it can. I learned that the quality of mercy and the essence of emotional courage is rooted in the need for forgiveness. And I learned that is never too late to change habits.

I guess I learned something from my father after all.

When We Were Young

Picture this: You're at a park with your kids and you are enjoying a lovely afternoon. Perhaps you brought some sandwiches with you to have a little lunch. You're playing your own version of Red Rover or some other game that your young children made up. You don't pay any attention to the fact that the game has a pretty cavalier approach to rules and fairness. You are more focused on their self-anointment as the prince or princess of "The Land of Goodness and Licorice and other Stuff." You, as their father, represent the evil ogre that eats nothing but "poop and dirt" and is feared throughout the land. There is no objective to the game other than when you do find the lovely princess or handsome prince, you're not supposed to scare them too badly. After all, "you're gonna be a kinda nice ogre, Daddy, and not scare me cuz I don't wanna be scared, OK?"

FYI. . . bring a sandwich with you on your quest to find the princess and make sure it's the one with the crusts cut off. Otherwise, she isn't eating it and no amount of stories about starving kids in Botswana is going to get that sandwich down the hatch.

It's a funny feeling sometimes, being a father. More often than not you just don't have time to recognize the sensation, because you're neck deep in making sure they are not wandering into traffic or jamming peanuts up their noses. At first, I had a hard time identifying with fatherhood. I had a hard time coming to terms with the colossal responsibility of the role. I also didn't know what the hell I was supposed to be doing. I guess I can't speak for every guy out there, but for me fatherhood was a reaction: be nice to them, feed them when they are hungry, and don't let them die.

But where did it all come from? Where did my children get the courage to fight ogres and slay dragons with empty paper towel rolls? I was told that stuff like that was hereditary, but that never made any sense to me. Plus, I never really trusted people who said they see themselves in their own children. I always wondered what the hell they were doing looking for themselves in their children in the first place. I suppose it's not a bad thing. Just a weird thing. But when you sit for a moment and look at the way they fight or play together you start to wonder where they get the mental boundaries, imaginative capacity, or emotional dexterity to interact with one another. Environmental influences play a huge part, to be sure, but for me to recognize the resemblances my kids may share with me takes someone saying, "Oh my God, Rawlings! That kid is you!"

I don't know why this surprises me. I have recognized the children of lifelong friends and shake my head the same way others do when they see me in my kids. Some years back, I was traveling on business when I let a friend know that I was in his town and asked if he wanted to get together for lunch. He couldn't, because he and his wife were throwing a birthday party for their three-year-old son. "Why don't you come over?" he asked me. "I'll feed you hot dogs and cake and we can catch up in between playing Pin the Tail on the Donkey."

The second I saw my friend's son for the first time (he was barreling around the corner with reckless abandon when he heard that cake was being served) I recognized him as the offspring of the guy I went to college with a lifetime ago. And when this kid walked over to another three-year-old, blatantly took the cupcake from that kid's hand, and shoved the whole thing in his mouth, it reminded me of his father's swagger and ridiculous disregard for authority and rules.

I've also seen the four-year-old daughter of another friend stand on the back of a couch in a perfect pre-dive position, fully prepared to pull off a body slam onto her older sister. Were it not for her dad's quick reflexes, I'm sure there would have been a few screaming kids in tears pointing at each other, assigning blame. I've never seen my friend move so fast. It made me wonder where that speed was on the college football field. The really funny part was that the rest of the other fathers were just sitting idle, waiting for the child to make the leap. We were mesmerized by the girl's pre-flop concentration. It was like we were waiting on the gymnast preparing for her final assault down the runway to perform her last vault routine of the Olympics. In fact, we were all a little disappointed when her dad came to snatch her off the back of the couch, because I, for one, was ready to give her a perfect "10," whether she stuck the landing or not.

And lastly, some time ago, I watched with tremendous pride as the son of a long lost friend—a man whom I loved like a brother and who had died well before his time—stood up in front of his family and a small circle of friends to declare his hand in marriage to a young woman he'd loved since they were both in the fourth grade. He was wearing the suit his father wore the day he married his mother. I know this because I was at that wedding, too, about twenty years earlier. For some reason, that powder-blue, homemade outfit with a black bow tie looked a hell of a lot better on a good-looking, lanky twenty-year-old kid with a scruffy face than it had on his paunchy, red-headed father. But as I watched my friend's son walk his new bride back up the aisle after the ceremony, it was like hearing the bells of the neighborhood ice cream truck again and not quite remembering where I was. . . or even who I was. . . but just feeling tickled that I heard the bells in the first place and that there would soon be ice cream.

My son has an extremely sharp mind, and not just for an eighteen-year-old. Of course I'm biased, but anyone who can write—at the tender age of eight—"In dreams I see, I dream to be, alone on a beach, just dad and me," has an intellectual depth that really can't be taught. I've quietly discarded the fact that he left his younger sister somewhere *other* than on the beach with the two of us, and gently appreciated that he had such a loving thought of me in the first place. And when my amazing sixteen-year-old daughter was five, she explained to me that all she wanted to be when she grew up was a doctor for tigers and lions and if they were hurt she would give them gum to calm them down. It makes me think there is *no way* either of these two beautiful souls got that kind of tenderness from me. And while their mother is a very intelligent, talented, and caring woman with a touch of the poet in her, I'd venture to say that she wasn't thinking such poignant thoughts at such a young age either.

All of this evolutionary wonder gives me hope that my children may have a grander plan woven into their fabric than I have imparted to them through my muddied DNA. That grander plan that makes me consider that the world isn't going to hell in a handcart. And when I see the children of my friends exude glimmers of their parents' amazing qualities—qualities that I respected, appreciated, and loved years ago and continue to admire today—it provides something far greater than confidence or trust: it gives me faith. It conveys to me a deep-seated belief that while I may not be around for every scraped knee, bloody nose, or broken heart that my kids experience, I know there will always be something embedded into their core infrastructure that will guide them toward a harmonious partnership with life.

So whether they come back from their quest through the Land of Goodness and Licorice happily ensconced in victory, or crying, missing a shoe, and with a mouth full of what I can only hope is mud, I know they will live and play another day.

When you really think about it, it's all this not-so-scary ogre can ask for.

Vowels

I am sure there was a turning point in my young life where I started to understand the significance of using some words versus using others and, more importantly, using them correctly and in the right context. I'm not sure when that was, exactly. Maybe it was when I was in elementary school and heard a neighborhood bully call a big pile of dog shit on the sidewalk a "teamin' pile of banure" rather than a steaming pile of manure. It didn't sound right to me at the time, but five days out of the week this kid wore a Black Sabbath concert T-shirt, not to mention that he appeared to be three or four years older than me despite being in the same grade. Correcting his vocabulary didn't strike me as the healthiest choice I could have made that day. So. . . there it lay: a big "teamin' pile of banure."

I definitely remember, however, how I felt when I thought I used the right letters within words. It was in third grade, when Mrs. Santamaria put cherry-smelling stars at the top of my paper if I got my spelling right, which I never really did but she was a sweet old gal and probably took pity on the squatty little mid-year transfer student with the hand-me-down clothes, Goodwill shoes (that turned out to be women's loafers), and the occasional, unexplained bruise. To this day, I still think "depot" is spelled "depoe" because Mrs. Santamaria said it was okay to spell it that way.

Maybe I discovered the significance of words and letters when I was twelve and reading the entire Hardy Boys mystery series. It wasn't until *The Bombay Boomerang* that I realized I was reading the same freaking story over and over again. I vividly recall the moment. I closed the book halfway through it, looked at the back and front covers like they were covered in dog slobber, and flipped it into a pile of dirty clothes in the corner of my room.

It wasn't out of disgust for the writing. Those books helped form my imagination and taught me that loyalty to friends is a precious gift, one that I would struggle with later in my life when things got hard. I just couldn't take the same cookie cutter template over and over again. I liked a good mystery as much as the next kid, but it all became too predictable. Mysteries shouldn't be that predictable. Besides, what kind of parents would let their sons and their sons' cheesy friends go tromping around after every perceived injustice in town? And what kind of area were they living in anyway? How many jewel thieves, bank robbers, and international "no-gooders" need to pass through the same small town before the FBI starts to take notice and puts up a road block or something?

Good thing it was the fictional 1920s and '30s. If Frank and Joe Hardy had grown up in the same small town I did, they wouldn't have had a chance to catch those ruffians who heisted the payroll at the logging camp, because those sonsabitches would have been found, shanked, and left for dead somewhere along the side of Lost Lake Road.

Letters formed words, and words shaped my future and who I was becoming and—more importantly—what I was escaping. For as long as I can remember, I recall being drawn in by the words people use and how they employed them to get their message out for social consumption. I wanted to be able to use the right words at the right time because, despite the aforementioned tough town in which I was raised, I didn't have the fighting spirit to defend either myself or our turf from the yuppies from the state capital twenty miles away looking for trouble (and our cute local girls). While fisticuffs only happened a few times (sometimes—back there and back then—you couldn't avoid a fight even if you wanted to) I just didn't have it in me to default to force.

Ultimately, resorting to violence to prove my manhood or to get people to like or respect me seemed counterproductive. And since I had enough of it at home, I tried to escape physical confrontations and lean on phrases instead. Within words, I found a less lethal way to escape the obscurity of poverty and the cycle of abuse that seems to tag along with it.

My kids are now in their teens, but when they were little snappers I used to sit them on my lap in front of the computer screen. I increased the font size up to 48, changed the color from black to red or blue, and let them bang away on the keyboard. They saw firsthand that they had the power to make letters appear. I sounded out the letters for them. I helped them type out their names. And at the very tender age of three or four, I introduced them (offhandedly) to onomatopoeia, which is the formation of a word from the sound it is imitating (oink, buzz, sizzle, etc.).

I don't know if that did anything to make them like words the way I did. I was just trying to spend time with them and—in the moments I had available to me—capture their attention before they grew up and became teenagers and explorers of their own. Maybe it stuck a little. Morgan wrote a fifty thousand word book when she was twelve, and Max has expressed an interest in teaching literature. It makes me proud to be sure, but I just don't have the heart to tell them that those jobs don't pay jack shit. That's the kind of thing they'll need to discover on their own, I guess.

Vowels, the very building blocks of the English language, held special significance to me. Not in the academic way toward the creation of the words themselves, but rather in the imagery they represent. For the record, A, E, I, O, and U are the vowels. There is no "and sometimes Y." Whoever told you that was just being lazy. Y was lumped in because *sometimes* it sounds like a vowel. (My, hyphen, etc.) Hell, if I used that rationale each time I was making a rule, my kids would have eaten one thing their entire life: beef stroganoff Hamburger Helper, even if they wanted soup or pizza. Beef is nutritious. Noodles aren't candy. "Stroganoff" sounded like a nice wholesome family meal. My point is that *all of the time*, I wanted to prepare them very healthy meals; *some of the time*, those came out of a box.

The sounds of the vowels were the memory makers for me. "A" sounds like "Aaaaayyyyy" which is, of course, the sound of Arthur Fonzarelli, aka "The Fonz." The Fonz was a character from the television show *Happy Days* that ran from the mid-70s to the early.80s. The Fonz was cool. The Fonz was smooth. The Fonz was the fictional personification of the real-life heroes of the 1950s: Elvis Presley, Marlon Brando, James Dean, etc. And whenever the Fonz wanted to get his point across, he would growl out a low, cool, smoky "Aaaaayyy" and look at the people he was talking to like they were all crazy for not seeing things Fonzie's way.

The Fonz (along with Evel Knievel) was the reason a whole generation of boys grew up in the late 70s and early 80s wearing leather jackets and wanting to ride motorcycles. The Fonz was a magician without the cheap theatrics and clown-like appearance. He could make things happen just by snapping his fingers or tapping them one time when he needed to. I remember seeing a real jukebox for the first time in my life. We were in a restaurant and it was sitting in the corner idly by the payphone, just like in the *Happy Days* TV show. And since all the Fonz had to do was hit the top of that jukebox to get it to play music, I thought for sure that the same magic resided within all of us. The manager of the place dragged me back to the table where my parents were sitting and explained to my father that he found this goofy eight-year-old smacking his decorative, antique jukebox and becoming increasingly frustrated when nothing happened.

To me, the vowel "E" will always be associated to the questioning sound of "Eeeee?" It seemed that no matter what book I was reading to my daughter when she was about a year old, her little finger would always find the tree on the page and look up at me to ask, "Eeeee?"

"Yes, honey." I would smile warmly and kiss the top of her head as I turned the page. "That is a tree. You're so smart." I thought I had a prodigy on my hands. I started thinking that the Leapfrog devices we were shelling out hundreds of dollars for were paying off. I beamed brightly while images of Harvard Medical School flashed before me. In my lap was a little brown-eyed girl who would discover the cures for the deadliest diseases, unlock the secrets of the universe, or reveal mathematic formulas that would change human history. I fast-forwarded to a future where I envisioned sitting among heads of state and other world dignitaries as my daughter strolled up to the podium to take the oath of office as President of The United States of America or to accept the Nobel Prize for Everything. But then she pointed to the dog and said, "Eeee?" Tucker, our yellow lab, looked lazily at both of us as if to say, "Sorry, pal. I've got nothin'."

The vowel "I" was I. It's a dangerous little letter that encapsulates the regret I have had over the last decade as I reflected on the emotional damage I caused to the people I love. I justified. I rationalized. I compromised to the point of complete separation from the things in my life that I—paradoxically—hold so dear. I. . . I. . . I. . . I am ashamed of the man I became.

Now I am working on unfolding the layers of denial and selfishness to get back to good. It may be too late in certain circumstances. For a while, my friendships with those I truly loved were scorched-earth campaigns and self-aggrandizing avalanches of narcissism that probably left a few of those souls regretting they ever met me. *I* took all *I* could. *I* drank all *I* could. And then *I* slipped out the back door in the middle of the night so they didn't see my shame and weakness come sunrise. That "I" has cost me so very much. And so it is the "I" that has to be repaired in order to get back in front of "You" to ask for forgiveness.

And so the vowel "U" is you. You are my son and daughter. You are the most important people with whom I wish to reconnect. You are the ones with whom I wish to restore the faith that you perhaps held in me when you were too young to know what faith was. You are my wife, whom I love and honor so incredibly much. You have always had the uncanny ability to look past the creases and the folds and the layer upon layer of rationalization to see, deep underneath, the brokenness of a good man just trying to find his way home. You are my ex-wife who probably has more reason and right to hate me than anyone else, but still don't, for some graceful, unknown reason. You are my mother, sister and brother, whom I have taken for granted and, at times, flat-out ignored because I had this misconception that I didn't deserve to be next to you. I thought I had to go to all corners of the globe to find what you had for me in abundance all along: unconditional love and support. You are the men and women who may have once, without hesitation, called me a friend, but now shake your heads angrily, or pitifully, or both and say, "At his worst, that man is a bastard. But at his best. . . *oh, at his best. . .* he is *so* very good."

And lastly, the vowel "O" represents the sound I have been making a lot lately. It has become the most therapeutic letter in my life. It represents surprise and sensation, acknowledgement and acceptance, the gentle release of forgiveness and the emotional wonder that comes with it. I am realizing that the mind, soul, and heart have all synched up to form the more perfect union of who I am now, versus the man I have longed to become my entire life. I've approached the letter and the sound from every angle and in the context of every emotion. From "Uh oh" to "Oh no" to "Oh, you did not just do that" to "Oh, I'm so sorry" and finally to "Oh. . . I understand. I get it now."

The vowel and the emotion it elicits has carved out for me a spectrum in which I can approach grace and wonder with confidence rather than timidity. I feel this vowel keenly, and I sense it will have a unique and redeeming quality in the years I have left. John Muir wrote, "Oh, these vast, calm, measureless mountain days, days in whose light everything seems equally divine, opening a thousand windows to show us God." Perhaps he liked that vowel, too.

So I have engaged in getting behind, beneath, alongside of, and within the vowels of my life. It is there I will find the details of the words to define the actions which will spell out happiness and peace for me. After the tearing apart and rebuilding of my life, they are the reference points and building blocks that will enable me to look back with a fresh sense of purpose and a more serene transition from chaos to harmony. And while I cannot promise there won't be some missteps with my intentions or some emotional slipups along the way, what I can deliver on is that I will have the right sense of direction as I venture out into the wilderness in search of forgivenss.

And that direction will be forward.

Game On

A few years back, I was listening to a local sports station on the radio in the car, I found out that at the Wimbledon Tennis Event in London two competitors battled for eleven hours of on-court tennis time. The entire match was extended over three days. The competitors were two virtually unknown players in the grand scheme of things. Both were ranked in the world but so far down the list that even the most ardent tennis buffs wouldn't immediately recognize their names. From now on, however, I'm sure you'll be hearing a lot about John Isner and Nicolas Mahut so put them on your radar. And while the sport of tennis was created around a thousand years ago, we should be more realistic and consider the audacity of this eventge in the context of the Wimbledon tournament, which started in 1877. Millions of tennis matches have been played in such tournaments all around the world since that time, but on the grandest stage of them all, two unknowns put together a heroic battle that will probably never be seen again in my lifetime.

As I thought about playing one match of tennis for eleven hours, I wondered about the longest sporting events in history. I've done some pedestrian research on the topic and came up with the following examples to illustrate how impressive Isner and Mahut's match is in comparison to other pastimes:

- Baseball: The longest recorded professional game was between the Pawtucket Red Sox and the Rochester Red Wings on April 18th, 1981. The contest lasted eight hours and twenty-five minutes. It was suspended at the bottom of the thirty-second inning at 4:00 a.m. by the league commissioner. At the time of the suspension of the game, there were nineteen people in the stands. Ten of them were passed out (it was $1.00 beer night at the ballpark), eight of them were vagrants because they saw the lights and thought it was a homeless shelter, and the nineteenth person was a woman who conceived, gestated, and gave birth to a son during the span of the game. The baby was called into the bullpen and asked to relieve in the twenty-ninth inning because the peanut vendor already gave up two homers to the men's room attendant. If you think I'm making any of this up (other than the suspension of the game by the commissioner) I'll validate it by pointing out that two of the greatest of the game at the Major League level played in this Minor League battle: Wade Boggs and Cal Ripken, Jr. Honest. Look it up. Or, as a friend says, "Google me, baby . . ."

- Football: In the longest game in college football history, Arkansas and the University of Kentucky battled to a seven overtime, 73-61 final score that lasted four minutes shy of five hours. For anyone who has played football—at any level—you'll know that playing this game for five hours is equivalent to being in a car wreck, on your way home from a car wreck, after being ambulanced to the hospital from a car wreck, in which your ambulance crashes . . . head-on . .. into another car. However, seeing that it was Arkansas and Kentucky, graduation statistics actually improved from all of the concussions sustained in the game. Ouch.

- Basketball: In 1951, the Rochester Royals and Indianapolis Olympians played the longest game in professional basketball history. The game took six overtimes and ended in the Olympians winning 75-73. The final score really begs this question: How in the hell can you play a game—during an era *before* a shot clock existed and with SIX OVERTIMES—and both teams only ring up 148 *combined* points? Answer? You have a bunch of non-athletic, candy-ass white guys with short shorts and high stockings running around the court passing the ball too damned much. God bless Michael Jordan, Lebron James, and the three-point line.

- Hockey: The longest game in NCAA hockey history was not a big-scoring contest, but those familiar with hockey understand that scoring can come out of nowhere and the real joy is the flow of the players. Quinnipiac University defeated Union 3-2 after ninety minutes and twenty-two seconds of overtime, in addition to the ninety minutes they played during the regular game. That is over three hours of "on the ice" hockey, folks. Three hours of hockey is like drinking thirty-seven beers and getting punched in the kidneys by all three Hanson brothers until all you piss is cartilage and blood. Disgusting and violent, you say? Probably. . . but so are the "drink-ups" afterwards. If you doubt me, go to a Minor League hockey game sometime. And if you are a sports fan and haven't seen the movie *Slap Shot* (see aforementioned Hanson brothers) starring Paul Newman, you ought to be ashamed of yourself.

- Boxing. This one is rather impressive. Seven hours and ten minutes between Andy Bowen and Jack Burke in 1893. They fought for 110 rounds and were only stopped by the referee when both fighters refused to continue. It was called a "no-contest," the equivalent of a draw in today's terminology. Both fighters answered every bell after each three-minute round. Both fighters scored so many punches they each were battered to the point of death. And both fighters were represented by Don King. Weird.

- Cricket. A long time ago, two teams played for a week and a lot of points were scored. Who really knows. Who really gives a shit.

- Soccer. Thirty-seven people died in the stands. Eight hundred million dollars of beer was sold. Final Score? Nil—nil. What a great sport.

All of these events illuminate one outstanding fact: competition, as part of a team, against another human being, or even internally against our own psyche, is a true catalyst in our development. We battle not only to win the match but to see how far we can go. We lose ourselves in the exhaustion of human experience. We mislay the compelling nature of competition and focus only on the potential victory before us. We fight for glory. We struggle for survival. We play to win.

If you question this, ask the Frenchman Nicolas Mahut who played over eleven hours of tennis only to lose by one point. He is not satisfied with being a part of his sport's history that may never be repeated again. He suffers not from exhaustion but from defeat.

If you still question the importance of competition, ask any NASA engineer in the 1960s how they felt when John F. Kennedy, in 1962, told America that we will "…go to the moon in this decade and do the other things, not because they are easy, but because they are hard. Because that goal will serve to organize and measure the best of our energies and skills. Because that challenge is one that we are willing to accept, one we are unwilling to postpone, and one which we intend to win. . . ."

Game on?

Play Ball

At the risk of sounding like someone not living in the now, I've had my fair share of highlights from my younger years. Unfortunately, it seems I have forgotten more than I remember. A doctor once told me that concussions are mostly to blame for the fog that seems to sock in the memories of my youth. I don't recall my first day of school. I don't really remember the houses I lived in prior to 1975. And I don't remember the first girl I kissed on the lips. That last one bothers me because that is something a man really should be able to remember.

The memories of baseball, however, remain. They not only have lingered in and out of my consciousness throughout my adult life, but they've hunkered down in my psyche for the last forty years. They lay safely tucked away in Sean Orr's back yard, Mason County's Little League fields, Shelton High School's raggedy-ass ball park and a dozen other fields scattered throughout the Pacific Northwest. The guardians of these memories were the superstars of my youth. They are the boys who taught me the game: The Hoosh, Kenny, Chad, Horner, Hoffy, One-Two, CSW, The Beave, Rive... the list goes on and on. My first experiences with the game and its glory were spent in their presence. The summer days of my youth were filled with a string of innings that lasted for hours, only interrupted by the parents who were afraid their sons had been abducted by aliens because they hadn't seen them since breakfast.

My days were replete with the sounds of the game: the shuffling of dirt on the mound or at the plate, the perfect ping the ball makes when it hits the sweet spot on an aluminum bat or the crisp crack from a wooden one, and speed of a fastball from the sound it makes as it pops into a glove or as it whizzes past your head. We learned at an early age how to ice sore elbows and shoulders. We could calculate, down to the very pitch, how much daylight we had before we were called home by a loudly whistling parent. If you left it up to us, we would have drained our fathers' car batteries to light the abandoned lots and backyards of my childhood. Playgrounds and backstreets were our battlefield. We were ball players. There was no way around it. We had to play.

It usually doesn't take much for me to think about these memories, but they have become increasingly acute when my son and I pick up the ball and glove and just play some catch. As with football, Max isn't keen on actually joining a team and playing the game formally as much as he likes throwing the ball back and forth. He asks basic questions about the rules, the strategies, and my memories of playing the game. As he probes to understand the rules, I shy away from trying to explain them and ask him to just appreciate the act of throwing and catching. Besides, the rules of baseball are ridiculous even if you are a veteran to the game, and if you are a beginner, they are downright baffling. For example, you can have two strikes on you and swing wildly at the third strike, miss the ball entirely, and if the catcher drops the ball you can try to run to first base only if there is no one on first base at the time. Here's another one: it's illegal to pass the runner in front of you on the bases. We can't just chalk it up to the fact that the lead runner might be a little slower or got a late start on the play. They're all just trying to get to home plate anyway, right? Who cares who gets there first? Baseball cares, that's who. And lastly—and if you can figure this one out then you're smarter than I am (which isn't saying much but I've played, officiated, or studied the game for forty years)—is the rule about pine tar, which is a sticky substance used to make the handle of the bat easier to grip. It is, however, illegal to have *too* much pine tar on your bat. Suspend reason for a moment and consider that it is exceedingly difficult in the first place, in the words of the immortal Ted Williams, "to put a round bat on a round ball that is going ninety miles per hour, and hit it square." But too much sticky goo is against the rules? And if you think I made that last one up, Google "George Brett/pine tar incident" and watch a grown man go ape-shit over the administering of this silly rule.

    Even with such dizzying guidelines, baseball is really just a game of simple exchanges. Back and forth, playing catch with your son or your daughter, tossing the ball between friends, and even (as I used to do) throwing a ball against a brick wall and waiting for it to come back to you. It doesn't matter if you say anything during the few minutes you spend in the backyard. It doesn't matter if it is mom or dad sharing the duties between sons and daughters. And it certainly doesn't matter if your child ever picks up a glove and actually plays a real game. It is the giving and the receiving that—at the very base level of human interaction—defines baseball.

Some of the best moments of the game are the unspoken communications between the participants. Baseball has such clandestine language techniques that you would swear it is designed completely by mimes. There are simple nods from one player to another. There are silent hand signals from coaches to players indicating when they should run and when they shouldn't. They are subtle shifts of power between the pitcher and the hitter that are recognized by a leaning of the body or the tipping of a glove a few inches in either direction. To the untrained eye, the game is mind-numbingly boring, but for those who appreciate the subtle shifts of power and preparation before a battle ensues, it is a strategic dance that can be the deciding point between errors and successes or between victory and defeat.

Baseball is also a range of odors so engrained in the minds of those who appreciate the game that one whiff of that familiar aroma can rocket a grown man back to their childhood to recall moments long buried and forgotten. Even after decades of inactivity or distance from the game, the smell of freshly cut outfield grass, or hot dirt on a local field recently sprinkled with water to keep down the dust, or the sweet, welcome bouquet of hot dogs and popcorn at the concession stand can whip the mind back to when those smells defined summer.

So, Max and I are playing catch. He is using my old catcher's glove that my high school baseball coach, Barry McKinnon, bought for me nearly thirty years ago. As Max was chasing after one of my errant throws, I picked up this old glove that my son threw at my head laughingly and put it on. I even squatted down in the catcher's stance and in an instant, I was that boy again. I was catching Chad's blazing fastball, Rive's wicked split-fingered forkball, and The Beave's "WHAT THE HELL WAS THAT?!" pitch. I was catching the fourth game of a doubleheader on a sticky ninety-degree August weekend. I was backing up throws, blocking the plate, and calling pitches. It didn't matter that I probably wasn't the best at doing those things way back when. It didn't matter that the games didn't mean anything in the grand scheme of things. We weren't playing for a World Series ring or for a national championship. To me, "way back when" was the small group of guys who taught me to love the game.

On that summer day with my son, I realized that I was a ball player again. And because my son and I were together, throwing to one another, back and forth, Max was a ball player, too. Of course, all of this was taking place as he happily ran after the ball that I lofted over his head. For all he knows, missed throws are a part of the game, which, of course, they are. But we were doing it. We were sharing the simple exchange baseball has to offer.

I was giving to him. He was giving back to me. Give and receive. If that is your definition of baseball then you're already rounding third base and on your way home.

The Other Guy's Resolution

A few years back, I was sitting on a stool in a little coffee shop looking out over the Willamette River in Portland, Oregon, when it occurred to me that it was New Year's Eve. Sometimes, a holiday gets lost in the shuffle of the preceding weeks and months and all the joy has been sucked out of the room by the time the department stores remind you what day of year it is. Especially when a Christmas or New Year's falls on a Tuesday. Really? Tuesday? I have a secret wish about heaven when it comes to the holidays. Thanksgiving is when the Native Americans get their land back, Christmas is in August and no one gives anyone anything but we all get together for hot chocolate and peppermint schnapps, and New Year's Eve always, *always* falls on a Friday night. Stands to reason, right? Wake up around 2:00 p.m. on Saturday, recovery takes till noon on Sunday, back to work on Monday morning. Easy peezy. But then again, it is heaven so maybe we'll have Mondays off.

As I was sipping my coffee I thought upon the upcoming year and how it could be improved upon from the previous one. I could lie to myself and blow a lot of smoke up my own shorts by telling myself I would take better care of my body, nourish my mind, love a little deeper, and all in all work a little harder toward being a better human. I have, in the past, made such resolutions and they have been carried into the New Year with the best of intentions. Somewhere between the best of intentions and August, however, these resolutions get their asses handed to them by reality. Overdue bills, bad breaks, another bout of whatever, one wicked left turn and just like that, the resolutions are left in the shitter. In truth, resolutions typically involve doing stuff I wasn't going to do anyway in order to feel like a better person for a total of—what? A few months? Then I'm left with having the same conversation with my psyche that goes something like this:

"*So . . . whatever happened to that resolution you made about. . .?*"

"*Don't you dare say it. Keep your psyche mouth shut.*"

"*About the resolution to . . .*"

"I mean it, you worthless piece of shit. You open your sanctimonious mouth and I will totally make a resolution to bust you right in the teeth."

"Why are you so angry?"

"I hate you."

"Perhaps you should make a resolution to not be so angry?"

"Perhaps you should blow me."

So, in order to avoid such an embarrassing existential scene, I gave some thought to a different set of resolutions:

- I resolve to not call someone a "douchebag" if they cut me off in traffic.

- I resolve to not intentionally cut people off in traffic, thereby invoking my own douchebaggery.

- I resolve to take the stairs whenever I can.

- I resolve to rethink the bowl of reheated chili at 10 p.m.

- I resolve to sing more in public and not worry about what the guy sitting next to me on the train thinks.

- I resolve to not verbalize my disdain for the Seattle Mariners until at least the All Star break.

- I resolve to allow myself one weak moment per month. The rest of the time will be spent strapping myself in and getting after life.

- I resolve to take a little closer look at my kids' eyes and listen a little longer to their words and talk a little sweeter to them when I can.

- I resolve to give others the benefit of the doubt even if they don't deserve it.

- I resolve to refrain from spending five dollars on a cup of coffee. Starbuckin' sonsabitches don't need my money that bad. But I bet the single mom in the espresso trailer at the job site could use another customer.

- I resolve to let go of what has happened. I am blessed to even have made it this far without going bat shit crazy.

- I resolve to appreciate the new "hellos" in my life.

- I resolve that I will make some more time for God. It's his anyway.

Maybe I'll keep these resolutions. Maybe some won't make it to Valentine's Day. And maybe some will become a part of me for the rest of my days.

But I do resolve to try.

Thunder and Flash

Nearly seventy years ago, a few hundred brave men sat terrified in airplanes as they labored and sputtered over the English Channel to the mainland of Europe under heavy German anti-aircraft fire. They were on their way to war. As the Nazi guns rattled them off their benches, blew holes in the other planes and scattered their comrades all over the coastline of France, many of these young men knew they were never coming back. They were the United States Army 101st Airborne Paratroopers. Their job was to jump through the night, land in the middle of three huge German armies, and raise as much hell as they could by overtaking German positions that threatened the success of Operation Overlord: The Normandy invasion of German-occupied France.

It was the darkest hours before D-Day, after midnight but before the dawn. The young men, not much older than twenty-two on the average, were laden down with every piece of equipment they could carry. The most oppressive item was the one, ironically, they needed the most; a thick canvas sack carrying a nylon parachute weighing nearly eighty pounds. Along with this, they were loaded down with the following gear: rifle, ammunition, wet weather equipment, small tent, first-aid kit, radio, flashlight, canteen, and rubber swim fins should the plane happen to crash into the Atlantic Ocean on the way to France. All totaled, the paratroopers had nearly 150 pounds of baggage as they waited for the light to turn from red to green indicating it was time to make their jump. At this stage, however, they didn't need a signal. The barrage of anti-aircraft fire rocketing up from below was blowing the planes to pieces. So bad was the carnage that the pilots of the planes were faced with three deadly options:

1) Climb higher to avoid the range of the anti-aircraft fire. This would have proved to be fatal for the jumpers as they would be dropping through the blasts from the guns below.

2) Fly lower at a faster speed. Also not the safest solution as it brought the planes closer to the guns.

3) Give the green light, regardless whether they were in their predetermined drop position. Get the men off the plane as soon as possible before they were all shot to pieces.

Option #3 was their only chance to keep the 101st (and the Normandy invasion) alive. The only problem with this plan was that they were nowhere near their drop zone. This meant that the men dropping through the pitch black sky (which was only illuminated by the bombs bursting around them) would be landing in an area miles from their rendezvous point and deep within enemy territory.

As the men jumped from burning planes, the impact of the wind ripping through their equipment as well as the shock of the gunfire blew all loosely attached items from their person. Guns, ammo, and even parachutes that weren't securely fastened, were torn from their bodies, leaving men either plummeting to their deaths or dropping into a dark country completely lost, blind to their surroundings, and without a weapon to defend themselves. Those who landed safely found themselves completely misplaced. Hundreds of men were cast into an eerie darkness, tens of miles from where they were supposed to be. They were in the middle of hell.

Their biggest fear wasn't that they didn't make it to their drop zone. Before they left the ground they had been ordered to memorize names of landmarks, cities, and villas on the chance that they might come across road signs. Under any other circumstances, it might have taken them extra time to get to their rendezvous points, but they would make it eventually. However, the most terrifying element of this situation was that they could be walking directly into an enemy patrol. As they individually and quietly made their way down ditches, along roads, through fields, and across streams—all in pitch blackness—they were ever cognizant that the snap of a twig directly in front of them could be a fellow American or a German soldier ready to shoot them down.

The only way of knowing who was in the darkness before them was the use of call signs. Call signs were secret passwords that were agreed upon and engrained into the minds of every American paratrooper before they went into combat. The American would whisper through the darkness a word and the responding word had to be the right one. If it wasn't—or, more likely, if there was no response at all—then it was assumed the Nazis were the ones making the noise in the darkness.

There were several of these call signs used by Americans within the European theater of operations during WWII. The most documented of them was fairly simple. The lost soldier would whisper, "Thunder." If the respondent didn't answer, "Flash," then they had to be ready to fight.

"Thunder." I am here. I am on your side. Please respond that you are a friendly.

"Flash." I am here, too. You are safe. I will not hurt you.

I've thought of this simple snippet of history often since I read about it years ago. I've thought how unique it was that in the midst of this global chaos there were instances of simple passwords that saved lives. I'm reminded of those times in my life when I've whispered out into the darkness ever so quietly and prayed that I'd get a friendly response. I'd ask, "Who is out there? Do you know the way? Do you intend to hurt me? I am strong, but I am also lost."

Some years ago, there was a response to my call. A voice whispered back that they were also lost. The voice sounded hopeful, but frail and uncertain. The voice asked if I knew the way. I replied that I didn't but it was still safe to come along with me. There was safety in numbers, after all.

So, along with this person that responded with the correct call sign, I ventured out into a hostile world looking for adventure and—at the same time—peace. Neither of us really had the tools to combat any opposing forces that we came across. We didn't know the way out of the pain that either of us were experiencing at the moment and certainly didn't have any map to outline where we wanted our lives to be going. All we had was each other to talk to, and laugh with, and bounce ideas off of so that we didn't feel like it was us against the world. And when it was time for that friend and I to part company, it happened as treacherously as it started; with the evidence of danger lurking and the threat of more perils yet to come. But for that brief period of time, I felt secure.

Nevertheless, as it was with the men of the 101st, a call sign brought me closer to safety during a dangerous time in my life. It introduced me to a voice willing to stand and fight and sacrifice its own well-being for mine. It won't be the last time I'll be in the dark, but if a simple word can cut its way through the unknown and echo a responding call then it certainly will be the last time I'll feel alone.

The Heart

My wife has an amazing heart. She likes old people and children, dogs and family, friends and French fries. She likes to think on things that can help those around her. Once she created a list of things that would make her Saturday "amazing" and the majority of them were things that had nothing to do with her but everything to do with those closest to her. She reads about medical advances and breakthroughs in the fight against the eroders of the mind. She knows what exercises are good for the heart, the hamstring and the hair. She knows these things because she cares about what happens to people and to herself. It seems like that is a pretty benign thing to say about someone and a simple compliment to make, but you would be surprised how often one's humanitarianism dissolves when one is tasked with being human to another.

My wife has a thinking heart, too. She doesn't just enjoy the stories of grace and charity she hears from her friends, from the news, and from social media. She embraces these things and learns from them. She moves herself into the portal of the literal—of the earthly—rather than wistfully ponder that she "should" make a phone call or "I plan on sending that thank you note." She makes a physical effort toward that first step which defines human interaction; the one thing that—I believe—will ultimately save us all. That is, she *interacts* with people. She calls friends, she writes notes of appreciation, and she embraces the opportunity to show that love indeed conquers all, but it can't do so unless it gets off its ass and does something about it.

Despite her courage and moments of action, my wife, sometimes, also has a timid heart. She has been present at and participated in emotional battles that I have seen ruin other people. She has stood alone in the quiet, clandestine spaces as she discovers that what she thought she knew and what she never expected are—at times—curious bedfellows. These revelations sometimes converge into a vacuum, and at that moment, lives change: silently if you're lucky, and painfully if you are not. Like an undercover agent of a secret army, she instantly recognizes what has happened, where she failed, and what needs to be done to make things right. It is a crushing awareness, and one that strips her heart bare of any of the defenses she spent a lifetime erecting. In those moments, at the end of the siege and the beginning a new journey, my wife's heart quietly lies open, vulnerable to the perils of humanity. But rather than running away or cowering in the darkness she steps out into the sunlight, opens her arms with her palms to the sky, and quietly invites the presence of grace. She knows her next steps may destroy her, but she chooses to believe that goodness triumphs over bitterness. . . even when it doesn't.

My wife has a heart that is fueld by the visions of a family life. It is a life that lies at the end of a long driveway with a house surrounded by tall trees and a prosperous garden. It was the house her kids remembered the most, the one to which they came home from proms and had sleepovers with friends. It was the home where she planted flowers and had birthday celebrations, Christmas mornings, and graduation dinners. It was where her children slept peacefully for years. It was home to them all and even when it wasn't anymore it became a damn good example of what home was supposed to look like.

The colors of her home were so warm and welcoming. She didn't know how to paint walls properly so—as she was prone to do—she studied. She learned. She knew that a home must have color in every room. Every corner needed something. Her walls spoke of the family she bore and the love she was raising. They were supposed to be walls of laughter and bonding. "I would write about the geology of painted walls," she once told me. "I would give a story to the strata of colors beneath the white. How covering over doesn't erase a life. Brush strokes with fresh paint only serve to insulate and lock in existence. My truth and my message would be to dig deep and look under the surface because in extravagant and simple ways, I believe everyone is merely trying to say, 'I was here.'"

I understand you, my love. I hear your voice and respect it. It is worth something very precious to me.

My wife's heart likes me, when it seems not many others do, or ever did. It's not necessarily a self-deprecating stance as much as a reflection on her ability to wade through the inconsequential to get to the substantial. She sees the boundaries and barbed wire I have put up over the years to keep a natural, simple happiness from trespassing on the vast acreage of a damaged life. In recognizing these boundaries, she has—in one breathtaking moment—shown me that the fences were actually keeping the poison confined within. She sifted through the rubble I created. And like water that falls on pavement and finds its way into every crack and fissure, she found me in a locked vault, buried deep within my own regret and shame; shivering, confused, and alone.

    I have been blessed by so many wonderful things in my life. I have been on adventures and lived through experiences that many others only read about in books or watch on television. I have also been beat down by life and have lived through the hard repercussions that come with willingly walking down dark alleys. The one constant in all of this is that there always has been a part of me that has been on the lookout for that heart that can cut through the storm clouds to discover the man that existed behind all the risk, the ups and downs. I don't know if it was my wife's destiny to make that discovery, but I know it was certainly mine to be discovered by her.

Every Breath You Take

My father is slumped over in a shaggy recliner. Both armrests are teetering precariously off to the side and the upholstery is fraying madly in all directions. It is nearly 2:00 a.m. and the rest of the house is quiet and its residents are hours from waking. The soft humming and rhythmic hiccupping of a portable nebulizer are the only signs of life in the dark little cave of a room. There is a small television on the metal desk in front of the man. During his retirement years and throughout his brighter days, it was his conduit to the outside world. He kept fishing shows, automobile auctions, and old-time westerns on a constant loop. Now, the box serves as a distraction to the reality of what is happening to him; white noise against the approaching blackness.

A plastic mask covers his nose and mouth as a fine mist of medicine gets whispered into his lungs at regular intervals by the purring machine that sits under the desk. The only sign that he is still alive is the sudden twitch he gives during a fitful sleep. The dosages of morphine that have been prescribed to him have faithfully done what they have been called to do: keep him painless and wading in a shallow, therapeutic pool of unconsciousness; not quite asleep, not quite awake, and all within sight of the end that lies before him.

This small back room of the old house is my father's sanctuary. It's been his refuge for over a decade. It was once dedicated as the laundry room and rear mudroom entrance from the backyard. Many years ago, however, my mother laid down the law. There would be no more smoking in the house. The grandchildren and great-grandchildren were now frequent visitors and she didn't want them crawling through a cloud of cigarette smoke. He put up a modest protest to his wife of fifty years—he asked not to be banished to the garage but rather to turn the backroom into his "office." She agreed and ever since that peaceful accord, the backroom has been his retreat from family drama of screaming grandchildren, annoying phone calls from solicitors, and the occasional Jehovah's Witness who knocks on the front door on Saturday mornings looking to save his soul.

Recently, I sat with him in this backroom as he dozed off to sleep. I watched him struggle for breath under the aerosol mask. He inhaled sharply, gasped for oxygen, and then, in a fitful rebuke of the forced air from the nebulizer, started coughing so violently that it seemed his fragile chest would cave in upon itself. After a few tortured seconds, he recovered a more stable pace of breathing, spat remnants of dark-colored discharge into one of a dozen soiled handkerchiefs he had strewn about on the desk before him, and closed his eyes to regain what was left of his strength.

The house is where I was raised. And the back room is the place where he took some of his last gulps of oxygen before the cancer that saturated his body finally killed him. My father had been all things to me during my life: drill sergeant, coach, role model, mystery, monster, an informational resource on auto mechanics that no website on the internet could equal, and lastly, a testament to the existence of compassion and grace.

He was also the beginning of my understanding of power. Based on his example, when I was eighteen years old, I thought that power was lording over that which you can control and manipulate for personal gain. As I grew older, however, I discovered that the true meaning of power was knowing when to wield it, when not to, and when to leave a little of it on the table. As I gazed upon this dying man fighting for every breath, I appreciated all the lessons in power that I came across in my days.

Power isn't just a decision made and acted upon at the expense of others. Sometimes—often—it's the punch Muhammed Ali didn't throw at George Foreman as Foreman was falling to the canvas. Power is the father who lets his young son run himself ragged at a jobsite before he steps in to demonstrate a more efficient way of doing the task. Power is knowing when to be silent and when to speak up, when to be still and when to move into the path of confrontation for a friend. When I left that house after graduating high school, I thought power was synonymous with control. I thought it was all about influence; who had it, who didn't have it, and what happens to you when you lose it.

But as I sat in the back room of the house where so many good times (and nightmares) occurred and held the hand of a man who held so much power over me as a boy, I found out that true power isn't about influence. I discovered, as the breathing machine hummed and the oxygen valves clicked, that the foundation of power is forgiveness. I peered through the darkness at this man and felt the last few drops of control he held over me seep through the cracks in the floor.

And yet, in some strange, unhealthy way, I wanted him to take his power back. He didn't look right without it. In fact, I barely recognized him. In that dark little room, I was feeling pretty powerful. . . and I didn't like that feeling very much. To break away from that sensation, I started thinking of other things. I used to think that when the end came for him I would ponder more meaningful topics. I thought that I would look back on our relationship together, harvest the positive memories, and reflect on them with reverence and appreciation, because he created several such moments in my life.

The man never missed a ball game I played in from the time I was able to stand to when I hung up the cleats in college. He videotaped games, hauled me and my goofy-ass friends to practices and summer camps, and volunteered whenever he needed to. And he didn't just do this for me, but he did it for my sister as well. He showed up for his people after putting in a solid forty hours at some pretty tough jobs. During that moment of weakness, I thought back on his appreciation and was grateful to him for it. I told him so, but he was too far gone down the morphine tunnel to hear me.

But even after recognizing these wonderful things that my father did for his family, it was hard not to contrast those moments to the ones that make me shudder to this day or wake me up in the dead of night over forty years later. Lord knows the man had his demons. There's no question about that. But I figured there was no sense in kicking him when he was down and at that moment, he was as down as a living human can get. I thought maybe I should consider the hardness of the man's life and how far he had come from his own broken childhood.

He grew up as an orphan on the streets of Toledo, Ohio and bounced between orphanages and family members until the Marine Corps accepted him when he was only sixteen years old. He didn't blame anyone for his troubles. He never complained about his upbringing or spoke of his hardships. And he answered his country's call to duty and faithfully served, at home and abroad, in peacetime and in Southeast Asia during the Vietnam War, for nearly fourteen years. I hoped that an appreciation of the toughness of the man and all that he went through would take center stage in my mind during his last few days.

All I could focus on, however, was his breathing. It's funny that with all of our history laid bare before us, the only thing that popped into my head was the simple taking in of oxygen and the blowing out of carbon dioxide. Up until then, I'd had only a passing awareness and appreciation of this physical act. As a former athlete, I've been breathless from wind sprints designed to push my body to the limit. I've heaved in oxygen while rounding bases or going from sideline to sideline on a football field. I've run stadium stairs until I couldn't trust my legs to keep me upright anymore. I have run for miles along country roads to make weight for wrestling. I have heaved a small tonnage of barbells until vomiting from exhaustion. I have held my breath upon questions asked, leaps of faith taken, and moments paused when time seemed to stand still. I have shushed out air in exasperation or hissed at ridiculous statements from strangers. I have made my breath whistle with song, blown out candles on a half-century of cakes, and gauged the temperature on a perfect, crisp November morning by the presence of my breath floating before my face.

In fact, I've published some pretty superfluous bullshit about being alive and full of hope, or have tried to define those rare, heart-skipping moments when I caught my breath over the wonder of things. All fine elements and sentiments that make for a decent Hallmark card and the modest sales of a few books (including this one, hopefully), but they really don't amount to a pile of monkey dung when the next breath you take may be your last.

But as I sat quietly with my dad, I watched him inhale and exhale and wondered how many times he'd done that without giving it any thought, and what he would give to have those easier moments back. I listened to the nebulizer feed my father what he needed to stay alive, and at the same time, came to the aching conclusion that that little box and the plastic mask it came with weren't going to make a damn bit of difference in the long run. The poison was already in the woodwork; opening windows to let in fresh air wasn't going to save him.

I was still thinking on these things when I realized that the blackness of the backroom was surrendering to the dawn. Dad's eyes fluttered open halfway. He rolled his head toward me and gave me a feeble smile. I took his hand and gave it a gentle squeeze. He pulled the mask from his face and let it drop into his lap. He shook his head slightly and grunted something under his breath.

"What's that, Dad? I didn't hear you."

He shook his head again as if to tell me that words didn't matter anymore which made me wonder, at that moment, what did matter to him. So after he woke up a bit and had some water, I asked him if he was afraid of dying. I asked him where his mind went as he was told that there was nothing that could stop this from happening; not surgery, or radiation, or chemotherapy, or God. I had thought what I wanted to know was whether there was anything he needed me to do for him, but what I was really asking for was permission to be in control of his life and hold the same power over him that he had held over me as a boy. In the recesses of my mind, I wanted him to know that I was the man and he was now the child. I had the strength and he was the weak one. I wanted him to tell me what he wanted so I could either give it to him, bringing the score to Norm:100, Dragon: 0; or punish him for asking and watch him cry himself back to sleep, just like I used to.

He tapped my hand after I rattled off my question as if to quiet me and my troubled mind. He gathered his breath and feebly whispered, "I want you and your brother and sister not to worry. And I want your mom to be taken care of."

I choked on my own breath as I held back my emotion and my shame. My voice cracked as I nodded my head. "Sure, Pops. We're going to take care of Mom. Don't worry. Anything else?"

He managed a weak smile and his eyes softened. He looked me in the eye and held my gaze for longer than I ever remember him doing when he wasn't staring me down for something. He looked through me, perhaps to the moment he first saw me in the nursery, before he adopted me. Despite his condition, perhaps he saw me for the first time as a man and an equal. And he looked at me like it was the last time he was going to see his middle son, because, as it turned out, it was. Then he looked out the window to the new morning and exhaled softly.

"Yeah," he finally said. "Open the door, would you? It's stuffy in here."

Epilogue

A few miles outside of town, on Johns Prairie Road deep in the heart of Mason County in Washington State, exists a park surrounded by towering evergreen trees. There are seven Little League baseball fields at this park, each of them varying in size depending on what age level of the children that are assigned to play upon them. I was introduced to the game of baseball on these fields when I was eight years old. Every summer for over a decade my sister and I spent hours playing baseball and softball there. It's where I learned the rules of the game. It's where I was taught teamwork and a commitment to something other than myself. I learned comradery, brotherhood, and the exhilaration of victory as well as the nauseating sensation of defeat. And then, after all these lessons were still fresh and regardless of the score of the game, we'd all go out for a twisty cone afterwards at the local A&W.

I hadn't been to these parks in over thirty years. The morning I decided to visit them again found me as a middle aged man, a lifetime removed from being that spirited youngster who would terrorize those ball fields on summer nights and weekends. Only this time, there were no games to play. The park was empty and the only people on the grounds were myself and my wife. It was a cold October morning in 2017 and sporadic yet thick, heavy drops of rain threatened a downpour within the hour. I didn't have much time to come to do what I needed to do.

The road that veered north out of town and toward these ball parks is one that, to this day, I could drive in my sleep (and probably did on several occasions). It was a route that my Dad and I travelled a thousand times when I was a kid. Pops would drive my sister and me to our games and rather than be a supportive bystander while we played, he volunteered as an umpire. Sometimes, he wouldn't be able to watch me play because he was officiating another game on another field. However, the occasional opportunity presented itself when he would umpire the same game I was playing in, and since I was a catcher and he was almost always the umpire behind the plate, we got to share the same small space on the same center stage, participating in the same sport we both loved so much. We didn't always see eye to eye on the outcome of things, but to this very day there isn't a moment that goes by when I'm faced with situations where lessons of fairness and objective reasoning are called into play. Life has a habit of yanking people off of their moral high ground or away from their ethical center. And at some point during those situations, I've wearily looked around and found my surroundings unrecognizable. The only way I've been able to even try to walk my way back to familiarity is when I'm able to pull the files on those summer days from behind home plate with my father and draw upon some of the lessons he taught me.

For instance, during one game where Dad was umpiring and I was catching, an exchange between the two of us regarding his calls on our pitcher's balls and strikes became so heated that he felt it necessary to eject me from the game. I stomped off the field, throwing my catcher's mask and glove toward the bench, and in general acted like a spoiled child. Mostly, I was embarrassed that my own father had kicked me out of the game, but there was a very secret part of me that was embarrassed he was my father in the first place. He was often brash, uncouth, and loud. He didn't care what people thought of him and cared even less about how he acted in public. He was a man who possessed very little, if any, nuance. And he most definitely didn't appreciate foolish behavior. So, when he called me out on my own foolishness, thus embarrassing me in front of my teammates and friends, I sulked back to the bench, grabbed my gear, and made my way out to the parking lot.

I was still steaming mad when I climbed into the cab of his truck and waited there for him to finish umpiring the game I should have been playing in. When the game finally finished, I watched him talk to a few parents, shake a few hands, and make his way out to the parking lot. When he stripped off his umpiring gear, he stood outside to light a cigarette before climbing in himself. He nudged me on the arm as he started the engine.

"You played a good game" he mumbled.

"What? Are you kidding? I **would** have played a good game if you hadn't kicked me out of it. What was that all about? Your calls sucked. You were missing the strike zone by a mile. That pitch in the 3rd inning that you said hit the batter didn't even come close to him. You needed a new set of glasses out there today." I couldn't believe I was saying all of this to him. I fully expected a cuffing upside the head and was actually preparing myself for it. What he actually did, however, still surprises me to this day. He simply nodded and muttered, "Yea…maybe I missed a few calls today."

"Then why did you kick me out of the game?" I replied back at him, still fuming.

He took a long drag on his cigarette before flicking it out the window. "Because you don't yell at an umpire. Whether they are right or wrong, you accept the consequences of their decisions and you sit your ass back down on the bench. You accept it and take your lumps like a man." After a long silence, he leaned over to me as he was driving and gently patted my knee, "Sometimes, the calls don't always go your way, son. You don't always get what you want when you play this game. That's just the way it is."

The echo of those words from 40 years in the past were still lingering in the air as I stood in that same parking lot with my wife. In my hand was a small box containing a plastic bag and inside the bag were the cremated remains of my father. My brother, sister, and I had all received a portion of these remains to do what we needed to do with them to say our final goodbyes. My brother and sister took their boxes to a river out in the Skokomish Valley where my father used to spend hours fishing for salmon. They remembered fondly the days fishing with Dad, so for them – on the banks of that river – they let the past and a portion of his ashes go drifting downstream as they held each other and wept.

For me, however, it was baseball. My father was always there for me when it came to that sport. He drove me to practices, he volunteered his time after working long, hard shifts at the timber mill, and he relished the opportunity to talk about the game with me whenever I brought it up. In those moments when we shared time behind homeplate, I felt that in some simple way we were as close as we have ever been as father and son. And so I decided that at that park, "behind the dish" one last time, would be the place where I spread his ashes, tell him I loved him in the way that only he and I would be able to understand, and say goodbye.

As I opened the bag and squatted behind the plate, the raindrops started to get heavier and more frequent. I smiled to myself thinking that – at any point – Dad was going to "call the game" and tell us all to go home.

He'd done it so many times before, but he would always wait a little longer than the other umpires would. I remember him always looking up at the sky as the rain pelted his glasses as if to say, "Hmmm, the kids want to play so I'll give it five more minutes." Sometimes the kids lucked out and the rain would let up. Sometimes it didn't. Those are the chances you take when you grow up playing baseball in the Pacific Northwest. But on that October morning, a lifetime removed from being a player on those fields, this ceremony was to be called on account of the weather. So Dad actually postponed the game after all…the second the last of his ashes fell to the ground.

  I stood up and looked behind me to the image I had in my mind. I imagined Dad standing there in his umpiring gear like he had done hundreds of times when I was a boy. I saw his bright eyes peering out from behind his glasses, and as he would pull on his umpiring mask a rare, warm smile wrinkled his weathered face. I envisioned him circling in front of me to use a little brush to sweep off any dirt from the plate. This is typically the last thing homeplate umpires do before they announce the start of the game. I heard his booming voice deep within the vaults of my memory as he yelled, "Play Ball!" My eyes moistened at his image and this memory. And then…I kicked a little dirt on the newly brushed home plate, just to piss him off one last time.

  I took Teresa's hand and we ran back to the car as the skies opened up and the rains came to say their own goodbye.

ABOUT THE AUTHOR

Norman Rawlings lives in the *Great* Pacific Northwest with his wife, all of their amazing children, and an imaginary dog, Pearl.

www.ingramcontent.com/pod-product-compliance
Lightning Source LLC
Chambersburg PA
CBHW051404290426
44108CB00015B/2149